# Englisch für Reiseverkehrskaufleute

## *English in sight!*

von
Maren Baldeweg
Anke Litsche

winklers®

# Vorwort

**Erfolgreicher Englischunterricht für Reiseverkehrskaufleute und andere Berufe der Tourismusbranche in Sicht!**

***English in sight!*** ist ein handlungsorientiertes Lern- und Arbeitsbuch, das durch abwechslungsreiche *activities* zur mündlichen und schriftlichen Kommunikation in der Fremdsprache einlädt.

Hierzu werden die Lernenden in berufstypische Situationen des Reisemittlers versetzt, in denen sie sich mit englischsprachigen Reisenden und verschiedenen englischsprachigen Ländern auseinander setzen.

Jede *unit* bildet einen thematischen Rahmen, in dem Fachvokabular und Redemittel mithilfe landeskundlicher Inhalte und authentischer Materialien vermittelt werden. Grammatikalische Strukturen werden kontextgerecht dargestellt und geübt. Die englischsprachige Handelskorrespondenz wird an geeigneter Stelle angewandt; hierfür werden eine Vorlage zur formalen Gestaltung von Geschäftsbriefen sowie *substitution tables* zu den einzelnen Brieftypen bereitgestellt. Die Bearbeitung der *units* in der vorgeschlagenen Reihenfolge ist nicht verbindlich, da die Themenschwerpunkte unabhängig voneinander gewählt wurden.

***English in sight!*** orientiert sich an den Lernfeldern 2, 3, 4, 8 und 13 des aktuellen Rahmenlehrplans der Kultusministerkonferenz der Länder für den Ausbildungsberuf zum Reiseverkehrskaufmann/zur Reiseverkehrskauffrau und greift Anknüpfungspunkte der Fächer Spezielle Betriebslehre des Reiseverkehrs und Verkehrsgeografie auf. Englisch wird somit Bestandteil eines zeitgemäßen fächerübergreifenden Unterrichts.

Berlin, 2004 Die Autorinnen

2., durchgesehene Auflage, 2005

Westermann Schroedel Diesterweg
Schöningh Winklers GmbH
Postfach 11 15 52, 64230 Darmstadt
http://www.winklers.de
Illustrationen: Bettina Herm
Druck: westermann druck GmbH, Braunschweig
ISBN 3-8045-**5052**-5





50522

# Contents

Contents

## 1.1 The work of a travel agent

**1** **Have a look at the ad below.**

1. What kind of a person is the Bon Voyage Travel Company looking for?
2. What other skills are important for the job of a travel agent?

### BON VOYAGE TRAVEL COMPANY

London's leading travel company has opened a new office in Rome. If you are interested in furthering your travel career, you may be qualified for this exciting new position.

**Experienced Personal Travel Adviser**

Full-time position based in Italy, reporting to our London office.

We expect applicants to:

- be fluent in English and Italian, German or Spanish desirable.
- have a good knowledge of geographic and touristic facts of the Commonwealth.
- have strong negotiating and contracting skills.
- be experienced users of Word, Excel and computer reservation programmes.

Our customers rely on us for unique vacations – you can rely on us for an outstanding salary, benefit packages and great travel benefits.

If you want to share our success, don't hesitate to send your application in English to:

BON VOYAGE TRAVEL COMPANY
Attn: Personnel Department – 23 Bedford Street, London WC2E 9HR, England
Internet: www.bonvoyage.com

**2** **Think of examples of what these skills are needed for.** Copy the cluster below into your notebook and complete it with your ideas.

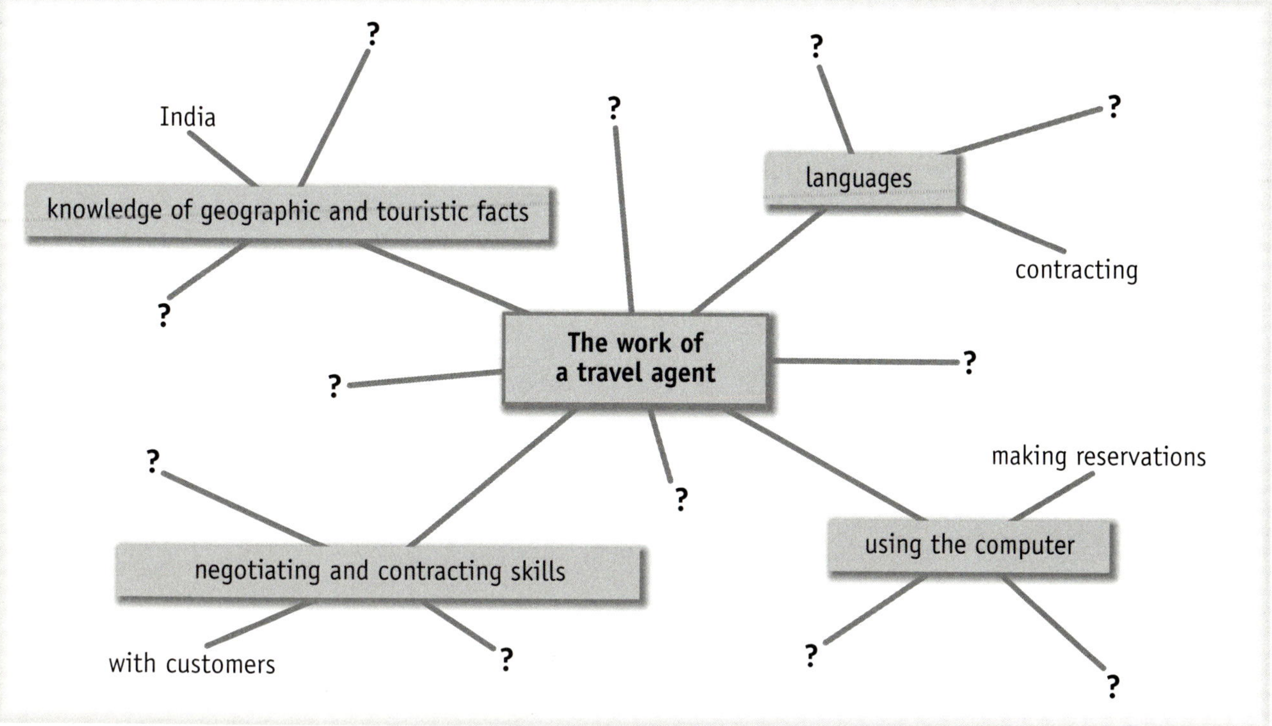

## 1.2 Travel agents and their business partners

*1*

**Work in pairs. Take turns in reading the following text to your partner.**

The listener should interrupt whenever a word occurs he or she does not understand.

Copy these words into your notebooks and look them up in a dictionary or ask your teacher.

### *Travel agents and their business partners*

The tourist's demands are met by a wide range of tourist services. These services are usually sold through a 'chain of distribution' the links of which are the travel agent, the tour operator and several producers of services, such as transport, accommodation and man-made attractions.

Producers sell tourist services in bulk, e.g. airline seats, hotel accommodation and coach transfers to the tour operator. The tour operator 'packages' these for sale to the tourist either directly – e.g. via the internet – or via a travel agent. This is where the term 'package holiday' comes from.

Travel agents arrange travel services at the request of their customers either with the tour operator or directly with the producer. Usually travel agents do not charge for their services; instead they receive a commission from the tour operator or producer for each sale they negotiate.

Of course, the business partners are free to make direct contracts.

*The 'Tourism Triangle'*

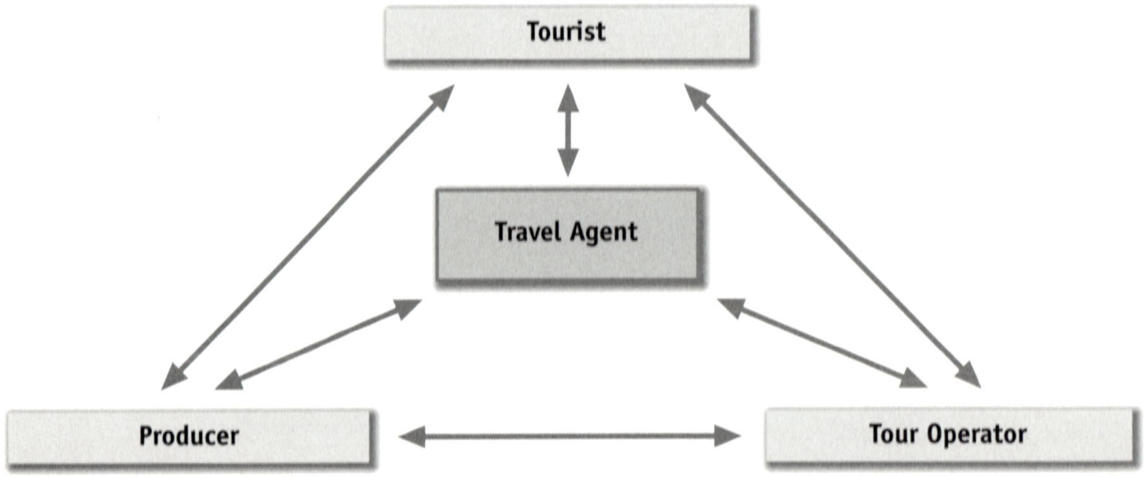


*2*

**Look at the 'Tourism Triangle' and complete the following tasks:**

1. Explain the 'chain of distribution' if the tourist wants to book a package tour to Cuba.

   What other possibility does the tourist have?
2. A tourist wants to buy a flight ticket to New York City. Where can he or she get it?
3. Producers sell different kinds of services. What are these services? Give examples for items that belong to these services.

   Model: *Transport → plane, private car, …*

## 1.3 At the travel agency

Steve Swan is the new travel adviser at the Bon Voyage Travel Company in Rome.
He sends this e-mail to his friend Cathy.

From: Steve Swan<steve swan@bonvoyage.com>
To: Cathy Jones <cjones@Bradford.ac.uk>
Date: Fri, 22 Jan 2001 15:39
Subject: Ciao Bella!

Hi Cathy,

Just a quick Hello.

At last I am in Rome! I work for the Bon Voyage Travel Company. Office hours are from nine to six but I have a lunch break of an hour in between.

Of course, most of my clients are natives, so I have to talk to them in Italian. Usually they want package holidays to India, Australia or the UK. First I have to find out what they want to do on holiday and then I have to find the best offer. Most information is available in brochures or catalogues, but sometimes I have to contact the tour operator or producer directly.

At the moment I am working on a special project: A group of Romans want to tour Australia. They don't want to go on a package tour, so I have to book their flights, accommodation and rental cars at the local producers. I am waiting for a positive reply from a tour guide in Sydney, too.

As you can see I am using the computer a lot; for reservations and bookings we have special programmes.

All in all Rome is great fun and I am thinking of buying a Vespa scooter which seems to be a must in Rome: People usually travel by Vespa rather than by car.

What are you doing? Are you still studying in Bradford? Are you planning to visit me in Italy?

Write soon!

Take care,

Steve

The text is written in the present simple and present progressive only.

| Tense | Used for | Example |
|---|---|---|
| present *simple* | facts<br>habits | Steve *lives* in Rome.<br>Steve *goes* to work every day. |
| present *progressive* | actions happening at the moment | Steve *is writing* an e-mail right now. |

**1**

**Read the e-mail again** and pay special attention to the tenses. Find more examples for the use of the present simple and present progressive and explain in each case why this tense is used.

**2**

**Practise the present tense usage.**

1. List five sentences expressing facts about the tourist industry.
2. Think of more expressions that people use when they talk about habits, e.g. *usually*, .... Write down at least five sentences describing your daily routine as a travel agent.
3. Look around in your class and note what your classmates are doing.

# Unit 1

## Office equipment

3

**Match the following words with the numbers in the picture.**

a) telephone
b) brochure/catalogue
c) travel agent
d) mouse
e) calculator
f) customer
g) photocopier/XEROX
h) wastepaper bin
i) computer & screen/monitor
j) filing cabinet
k) desk/counter
l) calendar
m) fax machine
n) map
o) printer
p) keyboard

4

**Have a look at the travel agent in the picture.**

Which of the listed positions does he hold? Explain why.

- trainee (BE)/intern (AE)
- manager
- assistant
- apprentice

50528

# 2.1 The history and development of tourism

1

**Let's travel back in time!**

Do you know the person on the left?

He is one of the first recorded travellers. He was only found in the Alps in 1991, but his journey already ended more than 5,000 years ago.

What do you think was the purpose of his trip?

☞ You may check the internet for further information.

For general information on the history of tourism read the text below.

## *The history and development of tourism*

Tourism is not only a synonym for travelling, but also a multimillion dollar business. All through recorded history people have felt the need to travel for various reasons.

****

The Egyptians were the first people to travel for pleasure. Travelling was also part of ancient Greece: The Olympic Games of 776 BC with athletes from all over the ancient world were the first international tourist event. Another phenomenon was the popularity of spas. It was mainly the Romans who travelled to thermal and seaside spas. These places offered not only sun, water and hot springs, but also entertainment and casinos. To make transport more comfortable they developed a network of roads of more than 90,000 kms.

Between the 4th and the 13th century there was hardly any tourism at all, except for explorers, such as the well-known Venetian explorer and merchant Marco Polo (1254–1324). He described his travels through Asia, which were received with astonishment and disbelief in Europe as hardly anybody could travel that far.

Medieval travellers took advantage of the road system the Romans had built: Religious travellers visited cathedrals and holy sites on special religious days – this is where the word 'holiday' comes from! As those trips on foot took several days, the pilgrims stopped at inns for the night. Later on people travelled by stagecoaches and spent the night at coaching inns.

In the 18th century it was fashionable for young aristocrats to spend a year or two travelling to the ancient sites of Italy and Greece. This 'Grand Tour' was part of their education. Another aspect of tourism at that time was a changing attitude towards nature. This romantic consciousness created the appetite for sightseeing. A view of the Italian landscape, in particular, was what people longed for.

The wealthy English and German families of the 19th century discovered the attraction of spas like the Romans had done centuries before. They travelled to places like Bath in England or Wiesbaden in Germany. The Industrial Revolution brought the invention of the steam engine. Now it was possible to travel long distances by train or steamboat. In 1841 Thomas Cook organized the first package holiday: a rail journey with tea & scones and brass music. Mass tourism was born and became an industry.

Up to the 1950s rail remained the common means of transport. Although the car had been invented before it was only in the next decade that it was affordable to the man in the street. The private car became the most important vehicle. From the 1970s on aircraft have become the essential means of transport. Destinations have changed over the past decades: First tourists flew to Spain, Greece and Tunisia, later long-haul journeys to Kenya, Thailand and the Dominican Republic became popular. Since today there is hardly any untouched spot on earth, tourists seek less challenge in covering long distances but in finding their personal limits in adventures.

2 **List the key events of each period mentioned in the text.**

**3** **Copy the following words into your notebooks** in the order of appearance in the text. The letters in parentheses will complete the expression below, if the words are organized in the proper way.

| | | |
|---|---|---|
| decade (D) | long-haul journey (Y) | destination (A) |
| spa (N) | stagecoach (L) | steam engine (I) |
| inn (O) | pleasure (O) | holy site (H) |

***'? ?  ? ? ? ? ? ? ? in history!'***

For giving information about the past different tenses can be used:

| Tense | Used for | Example |
|---|---|---|
| past tense | an action that began and ended in the past. | The ancient Egyptians *travelled* for pleasure. |
| past perfect | a past action that had continued up to a past moment we are talking about. | Medieval travellers took advantage of the road system the Romans *had built*. |
| present perfect | an action that began in the past and continues up to the present. | Aircraft *have become* the essential means of transport. |

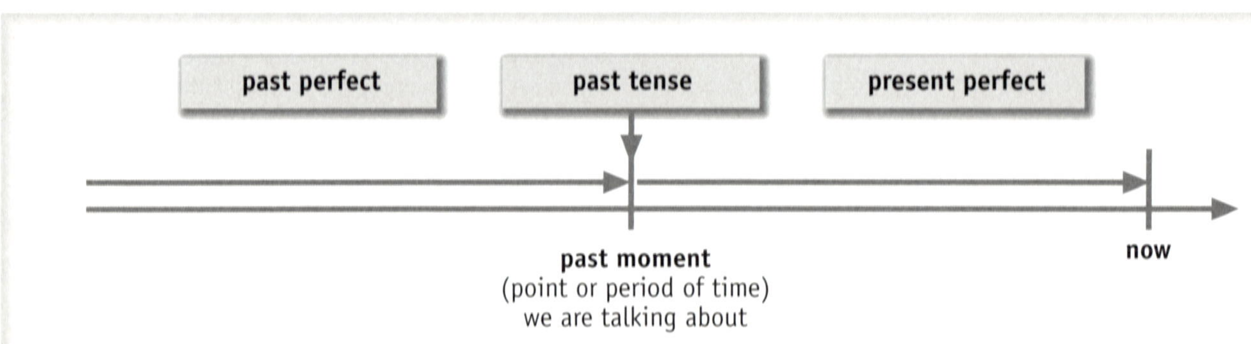


**4** **Complete the exercises below.**

1. Reread the text and find more examples for the tenses explained above.
2. Ralph is talking about his last summer holidays. Put the words in parentheses into the correct tense.

   'Last summer I (to go) to the US. I (never to be) there before. On the plane I (to be) very scared, because I (not to travel) by plane until that time. My journey (to take) me to New Orleans, Louisiana. This is where I (to become) a real fan of jazz and blues music. I (also to learn) to love Creole food. Unfortunately I (also to eat) too much fast food. I swear I (not to eat) a single hamburger since that time, but I (always to want) to go back to Louisiana.'
3. You have been working as a travel agent for some time now. Write a short text on what you have learnt so far. Make sure that you use the simple past, the past perfect and the present perfect.

# Future development

## *Travelling in the future*

'Space, the final frontier... These are the voyages of the starship Enterprise, its five-year mission to explore strange new worlds, to seek out new life and new civilizations, to boldly go where no man has gone before...'

Since tourists have explored every corner of the earth, people are now dreaming of being a member of the crew. Of course, this is only a dream but the first step into space travel has already been taken: The Japanese Shimizu Corporation has already planned a space hotel that will be orbiting the earth. This 64-room hotel will be finished in 2017. Its construction will cost about 35 billion dollars. Tourists will have to pay approximately 500,000 dollars for a package tour into space.

The trip will start with a launch to orbit, which takes about 5 minutes followed by up to a few hours of weightlessness approaching the hotel. Docking will be rather like parking a plane – but you'll leave the cabin floating along the access tube, holding on to a cable with your hands!

The project seems to be interesting enough that even major hotel chains are considering joining.

**5** **Would you like to travel into space?** Find pros and cons!

There are different possibilities of expressing the future:

| Tense | Used for | Example |
|---|---|---|
| *will*-future | actions that are *expected* to happen. | The company *will finish* the space hotel in 2017. |
| *going to*-future | actions that are *likely* to happen. | I think it *is going to* rain. |

**Notice:**
Sometimes also the present tense may be used to express future time.
e.g.: You *are leaving* immediately.
You *leave* at seven tomorrow.

**6** **Decide whether to use *will* or *going to* in the following sentences:**

1. I (...) travel to the space hotel, that is for sure.
2. There are no doubts, he (...) pass the exam.
3. Perhaps I (...) see a film tonight.
4. She (...) be back in a minute.
5. What (... / you) do tonight?
6. Mr Thomson is not in the office. He (...) call you back.

**7** **Write a science fiction story about space vacations.**

# Unit 2

## 2.2 Reasons for travelling

*1* **What do people travel for?**

*2* **Choose one of the pictures below.** Make a short personal description of the people (age, occupation, interests, ...) and decide what reasons they may travel for.

*3* **Now find out about your classmates and your teacher.** Before you start, make up a short questionnaire.

Keep in mind that there are different kinds of questions:

- open questions, using question words, such as:
  What? Where? When? Why? etc.
  e.g.: *Where would you like to travel?*
- yes/no questions
  e.g.: *Would you like to travel to Tunisia?*
- questions of choice
  e.g.: *Would you prefer to travel to Tunisia or Majorca?*

English-speaking people pay special attention to politeness. Therefore indirect questions should be used as well.

e.g.: *I wonder if you would be so kind as to tell me how old you are?*
*Would you mind telling me your age?*

*4* **Some people prefer package holidays to individual journeys.** Give reasons why.

## 2.3 Means of transport

**1** **Copy this chart into your notebooks and complete it.**

| | | | | |
|---|---|---|---|---|
| **mode of transport** | ? | water | ? | ? |
| **means of transport** | plane | ? | ? | train |
| **carrier** | ? | ? | car hire firm<br>coach company | ? |

**2** **Find suitable adjectives** describing the means of transport from the chart with respect to these criteria:

- speed
- comfort
- eco-friendliness
- price

**3** **Now compare the means of transport** using the adjectives you have found following the model.

Model: *A train ticket is almost as expensive as a plane ticket.*
*Travelling by plane is more expensive than travelling by car.*
*Going on a cruise is probably the most expensive way of travelling.*

Make sure you use the correct comparative or superlative form.

| **Adjectives with** | **Ending comparative** | **Ending superlative** | **Example** |
|---|---|---|---|
| one syllable | ~er | the ~est | quick – quicker – the quickest |
| two syllables with stress on the last syllable or ending in ~er, ~le, ~ow, ~y | ~er | the ~est | precise – preciser – the precisest<br>busy – busier – the busiest |
| two syllables with stress on the first syllable | more | the most | helpful – more helpful – the most helpful |
| three or more syllables | more | the most | expensive – more expen-sive – the most expensive |

Here are some common adjectives with irregular formations:

- good – better – the best
- bad – worse – the worst
- far – farther – the farthest
- little – less – the least

# Unit 2

## 2.4 The implications of tourism

**1** **Which implications of tourism are shown in the pictures?**

**2** **What do you think about the impacts of tourism** on the countries of destination? Discuss your views with your partner.
Use the phrases from the boxes below.

| Introducing one's own point of view | | |
|---|---|---|
| In my opinion … | As I see it, … | I believe / think … |
| I have the impression that … | To my mind … | As far as I am concerned, … |
| My point of view is that … | If you ask me … | I am of the opinion that … |
| It seems to me that … | | I am convinced that … |

| Agreement | Doubt | Disagreement |
|---|---|---|
| You are right, … | It is questionable whether … | I find it impossible to accept … |
| I agree with … | Of course …, but … | I disagree with … |
| It is undoubtedly true that… | However, it remains to be seen whether … | This is clearly a false view of … |
| … | … | … |

**3** **Who do you think is responsible for the problems caused by tourism?**
What can be done to combat the negative effects?

# Unit 3

## 3.1 Tourist information about Kenya

**1** **Describe the following situation.**

**Tourist information about Kenya**

**Capital:** Nairobi

**Population:** 17,000,000

**Geography:** Area: 582,647 sq. km. In East Africa, Kenya shares borders with Ethiopia in the north, Uganda in the west, Tanzania in the south, and the Somali Republic in the northeast. To the east lies the Indian Ocean. The country is divided into four physical regions: the arid deserts of the north, the savannah lands of the south, fertile lowlands along the coast and around the shores of Lake Victoria, and highlands in the west, where the capital Nairobi is situated. Northwest of Nairobi runs the Rift Valley, containing the town of Nakuru and Aberdare National Park, overlooked by Mount Kenya, which also has a National Park. In the far northwest is Lake Rudolph (Lake Turkana).

**Language:** Kiswahili is the national language and English the official language. Other African languages are also spoken, with variations of Bantu, Nilotic and Hamitic dialects.

**Time:** GMT + 3

**Climate:** Coastal areas are tropical tempered by monsoon winds (Jan/Nov). The lowlands are hot but mainly dry, while the highlands are more temperate with four seasons. Nairobi has a very pleasant climate throughout the year due to its altitude. Near Lake Victoria the temperatures are much higher and rainfall can be high. **Required clothing:** Lightweight cottons and linens with rainwear on coast and lake side. Warmer clothing for June and July and cooler mornings on the coast. Lightweights for most of the year in highlands. Rainwear advisable (Mar/Jun and Oct/Dec).

**2** **Complete the dialogue between Mr and Mrs Cusick and the travel agent** with the touristic facts about Kenya.

*Travel agent:* So, the two of you are looking for some adventure and a place to relax. – Mmh . . . Why don't you travel to Kenya?

*Mrs Cusick:* Kenya, that's in Africa, isn't it?

*Mr Cusick:* Yes, dear. You're right, to be more specific: It is in (1). But isn't it all desert there?

*Travel agent:* No, sir. The arid deserts are in the (2), but there are three other physical regions: (3).

*Mr Cusick:* So we can go on a safari in the savannah!

*Mrs Cusick:* I want to relax on the beach!

*Travel agent:* Don't worry. There are plenty of beautiful beaches and you can swim in the crystal-clear water of the (4).

*Mr Cusick:* What about the climate?

*Travel agent:* It depends on where and when you want to travel. Usually the temperature is about 30°C during the day but you should bring (5) for (6) and (7) if you want to travel during the rainy season.

*Mrs Cusick:* How do we get to Kenya?

*Travel agent:* You can either fly to (8), the capital, or to (9).

*Mr Cusick:* I heard that the national language is (10).

*Travel agent:* That's right. However the official language is (11).

Mr and Mrs Cusick can't make up their minds right now. They decide to think it over and to come back later.

# Unit 3

In the meantime Mr and Mrs Cusick have decided to travel to Kenya. They have returned to the travel agency and ask for more detailed information.

**3** **Read the information** and decide whether the statements following the text are true or false.

**VISA/PASSPORT:**

**Passport:** Valid passport required by all, no exceptions.

**Visas:** required by all except nationals of Denmark, Italy, Spain, Norway, Turkey, San Marino, Uruguay, Ethiopia, Sweden, Federal Republic of Germany, Ireland, Finland and Commonwealth countries apart from Australia, Nigeria and Sri Lanka.

**Validity:** Entry permits are valid for up to three months. Application for renewal or extension should be made to the embassy. Visitors pass issued upon arrival in Kenya.

**MONEY:**

**Currency:** Kenya Shilling (KS) = 100 Cents. Notes are in denominations of 5, 10, 20, 50 and 100 Shillings. Coins are in denominations of 1 Shilling and 5, 10 and 50 Cents.

**Currency exchange:** There is a fairly extensive hotel and merchant acceptance of major international credit cards. **Currency restrictions:** *Import*: Local currency prohibited. Foreign currency to limit declared. *Export*: Local currency must not be taken out of country. Foreign currency up to KS 5,000 or limit of import endorsed on passports. There is no limit to the amount of traveller's cheques.

**HEALTH:**

**Yellow fever:** A yellow fever vaccination certificate is required from travellers over one year of age coming from infected areas. The countries and areas that were included in the former endemic zones are considered by Kenya as infected areas. **Malaria:** Malaria risk exists throughout the year in the whole country. There is normally little risk in the city of Nairobi and in the highlands. Avoid swimming or paddling in stagnant water. Precautions with drinking water are thoroughly recommended. Health insurance essential. East African Flying Doctor Services have introduced special Tourist Membership which guarantees that any member injured or ill while on safari can call on the flying doctor for free air transport.

**TRAVEL:**

**Air:** Various airlines, such as Kenya Airways (KQ), Lufthansa (LH), Royal Dutch Airlines (KL), British Airways (BA), Air France (AF), Alitalia (AZ), Northwest Airlines (NW) etc. run international services to Kenya. Kenya Airways operates an extensive internal service including scheduled flights to Mombasa, Malindi, Kisumu and all inclusive tours to the game parks and the coast from Nairobi.

**Sea:** A regular international passenger service operates between Mombasa, the Seychelles and Bombay. Short distance ships sail between Mombasa and Dar-es-Salaam and Zanzibar.

**Rail:** *International*: The through train service to Uganda is suspended but a thrice-weekly service runs to the border from where there are onward connections by taxi. *Internal*: Kenya Railways Corporation runs passenger trains between Nairobi and Mombasa.

**Road:** *International*: Visitors from Europe travelling to Kenya by road are advised to enter by way of southern Sudan through Uganda or through the Sudanese/Kenyan border where roads are reasonably passable. *Internal*: All major roads are now tarred and many of the others have been improved upon. Petrol stations on highways. **Bus**: East African Road Services Ltd. provide bus services from Nairobi to all major towns in Kenya. **Car hire:** Cars may be hired from a number of travel agents in Nairobi, Mombasa and Malindi.

**ACCOMMODATION:**

**Hotels:** Accommodation in Kenya is divided into three different groups: town hotels, vacation hotels, lodges and country hotels. **Camping/Caravan:** There are no restrictions on camping in Kenya. **Youth hostels:** There are hostels in all major towns.

**Notice!**

As you know, one means of payment in foreign countries is the traveller's cheque. A forerunner of the modern traveller's cheque was invented by Thomas Cook, who also organized the first package holiday (see Unit 2).

Thomas Cook
Travellers Cheques
MasterCard

Today, Thomas Cook is a leading global travel and financial services group. Thomas Cook issues traveller's cheques in different currencies.

**Statements:**

1. Valid passports are not required by people from Italy.
2. Australians don't need visas.
3. Tourists can bring as many traveller's cheques as they like.
4. A yellow fever vaccination is required from travellers who have lived more than one year in an infected area.
5. The flying doctors guarantee free air transport for any tourist.
6. Kenya Airways operates scheduled flights to the coast of Nairobi.
7. Major roads offer a convenient way of travelling.
8. Lodges and country hotels are two different categories of accommodation.



505216

The text you have read before contains different degrees of obligation:

| Obligation | Advice | Permission | Prohibition |
|---|---|---|---|
| Valid passports *are required*. | Applications for the renewal of visas *should be made* to the embassy. | Members who fall ill while on a safari *can call* on the flying doctor for free air transport. | The import of local currency *is prohibited*. |

**4**

**Study the examples in the table above.**

1. Reread the text and find more examples.
2. Here are some other ways of expressing the different degrees of obligation:

   modals: must not, need not, may, must, have to, do not have to, need to, do not need to, etc.

   verbs: to recommend, to advise, to suggest, to allow, etc.

   adjectives: necessary, obligatory, compulsory, etc.

   Which degree do they correspond to?
3. Work in groups of three. Act out the dialogue between Mr and Mrs Cusick and the travel agent.

   Follow the structure below. Use the information from the text and the different ways of expressing the degrees of obligation.

| *Mr or Mrs Cusick* | *Travel agent* |
|---|---|
| Do we *need* a visa? → | Yes sir, you *have to* have a visa. |
| ← Are any vaccinations (...)? → | No, only travellers from infected areas (...) a vaccination certificate. |
| ← What about drinking water? → | (...) |
| ← (...) | |

**5**

**Up to now, the Cusicks have basically enquired** about formal aspects of Kenya, such as entry regulations and travel requirements.

What else are customers interested in when they come to your travel agency? Make a list.

Now the Cusicks are on their way to Kenya ...

# Unit 3

## 3.2 Tourist information about the Hakuna Matata Beach Resort

### *Hakuna Matata Beach Resort*

#### *Prepare to be swept away ...*

No matter what your concept of an ideal vacation is, the Hakuna Matata Beach Resort at Shanzu Beach, 18 km from Mombasa, will exceed your expectations.

For those who want an active holiday, Hakuna Matata provides the ideal environment with our excellent sports & fitness complex, and everything is included in one attractive price: accommodation, meals, snacks, alcoholic beverages, water sports, golf, tennis & fitness facilities with instruction and round trip transfers from Mombasa Airport.

From snorkeling and scuba diving to deep-sea fishing the crystal-clear Indian Ocean is yours. Enjoy our health & fitness programmes, including water gymnastics in our fresh-water pools.

The nearby village of Shanzu provides you with all necessities of everyday life, such as a drugstore & pharmacy, a bank & money exchange office, and nice boutiques.

The local tourist information office organizes excursions & safaris, but do not hesitate to contact your on-site representative as well.

**1** **Here are some exercises** referring to the vocabulary in the text above. Complete them.

1. What do the words in **A** mean? Choose the correct explanations from **B.**

| A | B |
|---|---|
| round-trip transfer | an employee of a tour operator, who looks after tourists at their holiday resort |
| | a sightseeing tour through nearby villages and cities |
| on-site representative | the transport from the airport to the holiday resort and from the holiday resort back to the airport |
| | a person, who represents the hotel staff |

2. Odd man out – Can you find the wrong word?
   a) snorkeling – scuba diving – water sports
   b) deep-sea fishing – water gymnastics – sailing
3. Find the right word.
   a) Beer, whisky, and wine are (...).
   b) A (...) sells tissues, suntan lotions, and toothpaste.
   c) Medicine, malaria prophylaxis, and plasters are sold by a (...).

**2** **What other sports and infrastructural facilities are usually offered in holiday resorts?**

**3** **Now explain to Mrs Cusick what her beach holiday will be like.** Work in pairs.



505218

## Going on safari: The Magic of Kenya

**4** **Before you read the itinerary of the Magic of Kenya safari** have a look at the photos and imagine what the tour could be like.

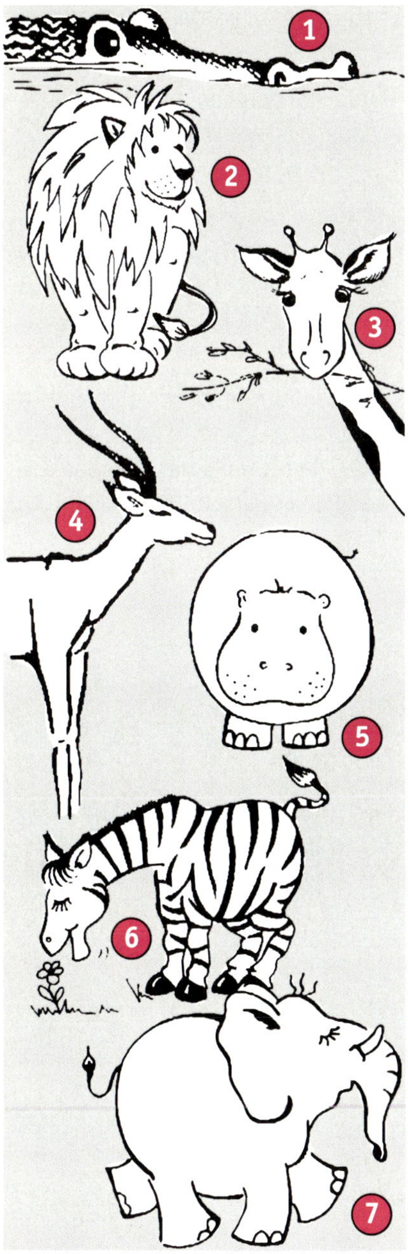

### *The Magic of Kenya*

**Day 1**
A bus takes you from your holiday resort at the Indian Ocean to the Taita Hills Reserve where you meet your native tour guide. Lunch is served at the Taita Hills Lodge. In the afternoon you come across your first wild animals, such as elephants, giraffes, and lions in their natural environment. Dinner and overnight stay at the Salt Lick Lodge.

**Day 2**
After a rich breakfast today's excursion takes you to the Amboseli National Park that is located at the foot of the snow-capped Kilimanjaro – the highest mountain in Africa. Around noon you reach the comfortable Amboseli Serena Lodge. After lunch you stalk through the Amboseli. Although a relatively small reserve, it is the habitat of a vast range of wild animals: elephants, giraffes, lions, hyenas, zebras, antelopes and others. Dinner and overnight stay at the Amboseli Serena Lodge.

**Day 3**
Today an early breakfast is offered before you leave for the western part of the Tsavo National Park. At lunchtime you arrive at the luxurious Finch Hattons Safari Camp. Stalk in the afternoon until sunset. Opportunity of achieving a closeness with nature you would not have thought possible. You have the thrill of viewing crocodiles and hippopotamuses at the Mzima Springs. Dinner and overnight stay at the Finch Hattons Safari Camp. Relax in the unique atmosphere and be enchanted by the colonial charm of this extravagant safari camp.

**Day 4**
Your last day starts with an early breakfast. Then you are taken to the eastern part of the Tsavo National Park. Stalk until lunch at the Voi Safari Lodge from where you can enjoy the beautiful view of the savannah. In the afternoon you are taken back to Mombasa. From there transfer to your holiday resort.

**5** **The names of some animals** you can see on the Magic of Kenya safari are mixed up. Reorder the letters and match the animal names with the drawings.

a) ebazr  b) figaref  c) olni  d) htnepale
e) latenpeo  f) rodcoclie  g) motpipusahopi

**6** **Explain to Mr Cusick what his safari will be like.** Work in pairs. Give information about:

- types of accommodation
- places to be visited
- kinds of meals
- animals to be seen

505219

This table shows how to express conditions:

| If-clauses | Used for | Example |
|---|---|---|
| Type I:<br>present tense + will future | possible and likely situations. | If you *go* on a safari,<br>you *will see* wild animals. |
| Type II:<br>past tense + conditional I | possible, but unlikely situations. | If you *went* on a safari, you *would see* wild animals. |
| Type III:<br>past perfect + conditional II | impossible situations<br>(did not happen). | If you *had gone* on a safari, you *would have seen* wild animals. |

7

**Study the examples above and complete these exercises.**

1. Decide which of the three types of if-clauses have to be used in the following situations:
   a) Mr Cusick wants to see wild animals. He talks to his on-site representative.
   b) Mr Cusick tries to convince his wife to go on a safari, although he knows that she is afraid of the wilderness.
   c) Mrs Cusick decides to stay in the holiday resort while her husband goes on safari. On their flight back home she complains to him that she has not seen any wild animals in Kenya.
2. Match the beginnings and endings of the sentences below.

| | |
|---|---|
| 1. If you don't get up at 5 a.m., | a) if you had used your suntan lotion. |
| 2. We would have slept well | b) you would not have been left behind. |
| 3. You would not have a sunburn | c) if I don't travel to Kenya. |
| 4. If you hadn't jumped off the Jeep, | d) you will miss your early breakfast. |
| 5. I will not find out how nice it is | e) if we had taken a mosquito net. |

## Presenting further countries

8

**Now it's your turn!** Work in groups and prepare a presentation of one of the following countries:

- South Africa
- Indonesia
- Mexico
- Maldives
- Thailand
- USA: Florida, California

Of course, you may suggest other countries as well.

Your presentation should give:
- geographic information about the country
- general tourist information
- information about holiday resorts and local tours

In your groups, discuss:
- possible sources of information
- possible media for giving a presentation
- organization of the work (Who does what and when?)

☞ Check the appendix for how to write an enquiry to the local tourist board and how to give a presentation.



505220

# 4.1 Some facts about air travel

**1**

**Have a look at these sentences** and decide whether they are true or false.

1. Aircraft have been a common means of transport since the 1950s.
2. People can book their flights at airline ticket offices.
3. Travelling on long distances may make it necessary to change planes.
4. Customers always have to pay a deposit when they book their flights.
5. Travellers have to be at the airport half an hour before take-off.

**2**

**Read the text below.**

1. Check if your answers to exercise 1 were right.
2. Try to explain the underlined words to your classmates.

## *Some facts about air travel*

The airline industry is still very young. Only during recent decades air transport has become a means of transportation that is just as common as bus or rail. If you want to travel by plane you usually need an advance reservation. You can book your flight either at an airline ticket office or at a travel agency – especially those who are approved IATA-agents. Passengers can choose between business, economy (BE) / coach (AE) and on long-distance flights even first class.

If you travel within Europe you will probably get a direct or non-stop flight, whereas on long-distance flights you might have to change planes and take a connecting flight. If this is the case your travel agent will have to consider the minimum connecting time in order to make sure that you don't miss the plane.

You can either book a single or a return flight (BE) / round trip (AE). In general, you have to confirm your flight three days before you leave. However, sometimes planes are booked up. In this case the airline or your travel agent can put you on a waiting list and if you are lucky there will be a seat for you later on.

Some travel agencies want you to pay a deposit when you book your flight, others just want you to pay when you collect your ticket.

Make sure that you don't forget your passport and get to the airport at least one hour before take-off!

**3**

**Match the beginnings and endings of the following sentences.**

| | |
|---|---|
| 1. IATA-agents | a) stands for *International Air Transport Association.* |
| 2. Direct flights | b) are travel agents with a special authorization. |
| 3. Non-stop flights | c) is the American word for *return flight*. |
| 4. IATA | d) may have stops on the way but the flight numbers don't change. |
| 5. *Round trip* | e) take you directly from one city to another. |

## 4.2 Giving information about schedules

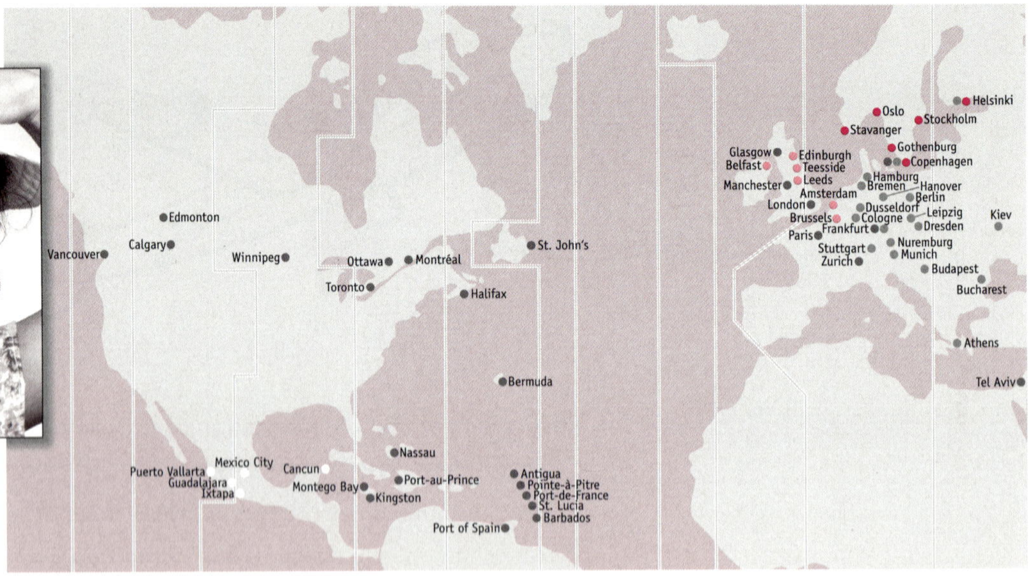


This is Teresa Burns from Edmonton, Canada. She wants to travel to Paris, France.

**1**

**What questions would you as a travel agent ask her** when she comes to your office? What could Teresa answer or ask?

Work in pairs. The information from the boxes may help you.

| | |
|---|---|
| What ...? | Where ...? |
| How much ...? | How old ...? |
| How long ...? | Who ...? |
| How many ...? | When ...? |

| **Teresa Burns** |
|---|
| single |
| 19 years old |
| student |
| 3-week vacation in June |
| wants to visit friends in Paris |
| ... |

The travel agent has gathered enough information about Teresa's plans and the conversation goes on like this:

*Travel agent:* OK. Let's check the computer. – Oh, heavens, it's not working! Well, let's have a look at the Air Canada flight schedule then. – Hm, yes, there is a flight from Edmonton to Paris.

*Teresa:* Is it a direct flight?

*Travel agent:* No, it's a connecting flight.

*Teresa:* Where do I have to change planes?

*Travel agent:* I don't know. We have to have a look at the OAG Air Travel Guide:

**Departure and arrival times**

All times are local times.
Times in **bold type** are the times of departures from the city of origin and of arrivals at the final destination.

Time in light type are the times of arrival and departure at each transfer connection airport.

**Direct flights**
If the times on one line are both in **bold type,** the flight is a direct flight.

It may go non-stop from the departure city to the arrival city.

Or it may stop at one or more cities en route.

Direct flights normally have the same flight number from beginning to end.

**Transfer connections**
If the times on one line are NOT both in **bold type,** it is a transfer connection flight.

The first line shows the direct flight from the departure city to the airport at which a change of flight is necessary. The last line shows the connecting flight to the final destination.

| Departure city name | Country | City code | Time variation from GMT |
|---|---|---|---|
| FROM **EDMONTON** | AL CANADA | **YEA** | **-0700** |

● INTERNATIONAL (YEG) 21mls/34kms S of Edmonton. Check–in 45mins except AA 60, AC to USA 60, other Int 90.

● MUNICIPAL (YXD) 3mls/5kms N of Edmonton. Check–in 45mins except CP 30.

To International Airport
BUS
Grey Goose Airport Bus Service from downtown Edmonton. Calls at major hotels. Journey time 45 mins. Enquiry tel: (403) 463 7520.

**Paris France** PAR — CDG-C De Gaulle

| | | | | | | | | |
|---|---|---|---|---|---|---|---|---|
| 2Jan | – | 1234567 | **1205** YEG | 1737 YYZ | **AC** 126 | 320 | JYMBH | 0 |
| | | | 2010 YYZ | *__0935__ CDG | **AC** 880 | 747 | FJYBH | 1 |

***AC880**Plane change at intermediate stop*

Labels (left to right): Date when the service starts; Date when the service ends; Days of the week when the service operates; Departure time (etd) and code of departure airport; Arrival time (eta) and code of arrival airport; Airline code and flight number; Type of aircraft; Class of service; Number of stops

**Day indicators**
The symbols in these columns show wich arrival and departure times are not on the same day as the day when the journey started.
* second day
‡ third day
§ fourth day
¶ previous day

**Days of the week**
1 Monday
2 Tuesday
3 Wednesday
4 Thursday
5 Friday
6 Saturday
7 Sunday

**Class of service available on the flight**
**First class**
**P, F, A**

**Business class**
**J, C, D, Z**

**Economy/coach class**
**W, S, Y, B, H, K, M, N, Q, T, V, X**

**2** **Answer the questions on the extract of the OAG Air Travel Guide.**

1. Where is the airport located?
2. How can Teresa get to the airport?
3. When does she have to be there?
4. What is the city code for Paris?
5. What is meant by *CDG*?
6. What does *AC* stand for?
7. What are the flight numbers?
8. Which types of aircraft can Teresa fly with?
9. Which classes of service are offered?
10. Does the flight arrive in Paris on the same day?
11. Does the flight operate daily?
12. How many intermediate stops are there en route?

505223

# Unit 4

**3** **Finish the dialogue between Teresa and the travel agent** in which he explains the flight details to her. Use the extracts from the AC flight schedule and your answers from exercise *2*.

Travel agent: (...)

Teresa: (...)

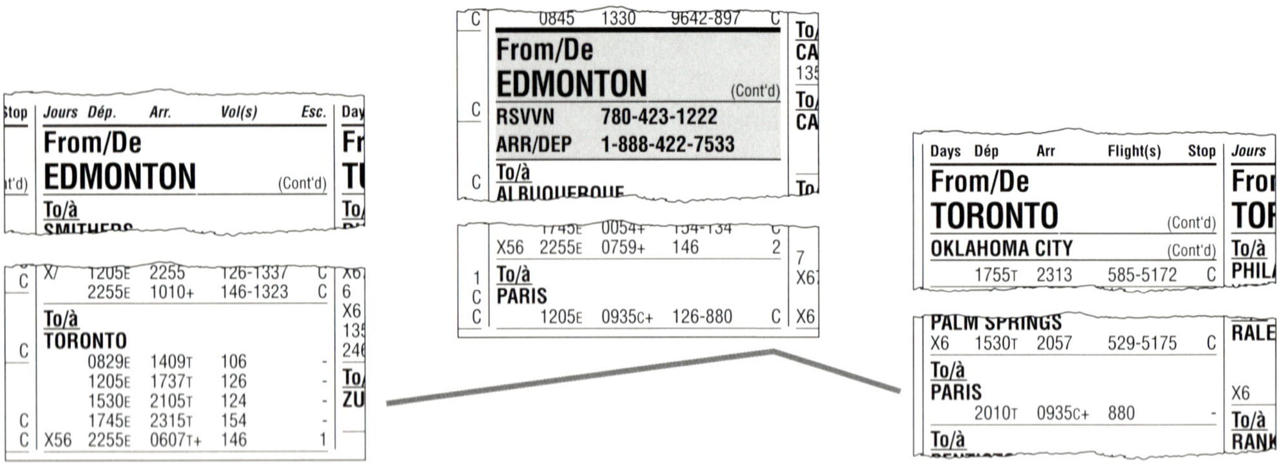

Stop | Jours Dép. Arr. Vol(s) Esc. | Day

From/De
EDMONTON (Cont'd)
To/à
SMITHERS

X7 1205E 2255 126-1337 C
2255E 1010+ 146-1323 C
To/à
TORONTO
0829E 1409T 106 -
1205E 1737T 126 -
1530E 2105T 124 -
1745E 2315T 154 -
X56 2255E 0607T+ 146 1

0845 1330 9642-897 C
From/De
EDMONTON (Cont'd)
RSVVN 780-423-1222
ARR/DEP 1-888-422-7533
To/à
ALBUQUERQUE

1745E 0054+ 154-134 C
X56 2255E 0759+ 146 2
To/à
PARIS
1205E 0935C+ 126-880 C

Days Dép Arr Flight(s) Stop | Jours
From/De
TORONTO (Cont'd)
OKLAHOMA CITY (Cont'd)
1755T 2313 585-5172 C

PALM SPRINGS
X6 1530T 2057 529-5175 C
To/à
PARIS
2010T 0935C+ 880 -
To/à

## Talking about time

**4** **Turn back to the timetable extracts.** What other possibilities of expressing the departure and arrival times can you think of?

### COMMON WAYS OF GIVING THE TIME

When giving the time in full, 'minutes' is often omitted when the number of minutes is 5, 10, 20 and so on. The hour may also be dropped if it is clear what hour is meant. In American English you can say 'after' instead of 'past', and 'of' or 'before' instead of 'to'. The abbreviations 'a.m.' and 'p.m.' are used after the times when it is important to be clear whether the time is in the morning or evening.

| | | |
|---|---|---|
| a.m. = before noon | **7.00** | seven/seven o'clock |
| | **8.05** | eight o five/five past eight/five minutes past eight<br>*(Am also)* five after eight/five minutes after eight |
| | **9.17** | nine seventeen/seventeen minutes past nine |
| | **10.30** | ten thirty/half past ten/(*Br infml*) half ten/(*Am infml*) half after ten |
| | **11.40** | eleven forty/twenty to twelve/twenty minutes to twelve<br>*(Am also)* twenty of twelve/twenty before twelve |
| | **12.00** | twelve/twelve o'clock/midday/noon/twelve noon |
| p.m. = after-noon | **2.01** | two o one/a minute past two/one minute past two |
| | **3.15** | three fifteen/quarter past three/a quarter past three |
| | **8.45** | eight forty-five/quarter to nine/a quarter to nine |
| | **12.00** | twelve/midnight/twelve o'clock/twelve midnight |

The 24-hour clock is generally used for railway and air timetables, though less often in America. Times are read simply as numbers *13.15 – thirteen fifteen* and the exact hours are read using 'hundred' *16.00 – sixteen hundred (hours)*.

**5** **Work in pairs.** Give information about other flights from the timetable extracts as indicated by the model. Make at least five sentences. Use the different possibilities of giving the time according to the information box.

Model: *When does flight number AC 154 to Toronto leave?*
*It leaves at seventeen forty-five.*
*When does flight number AC 154 arrive in Toronto?*
*It arrives at eleven fifteen p.m.*



505224

## 4.3 Ticketing

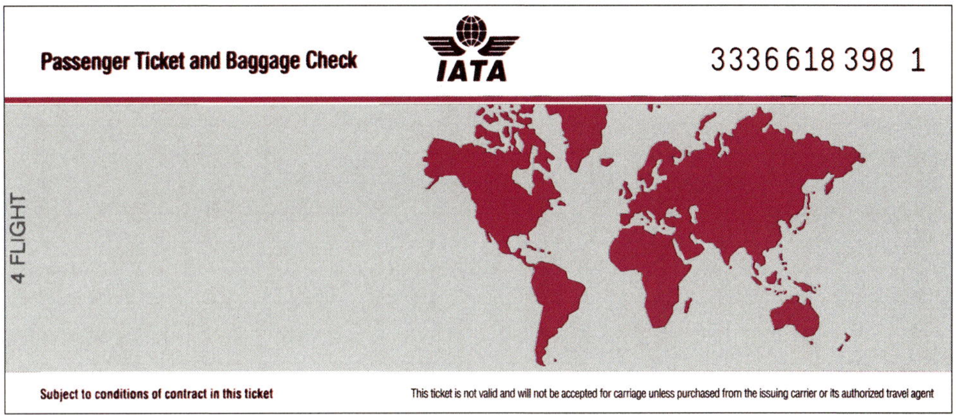


An airline ticket gives evidence of the contract made between the airline and the passenger. The most important conditions of carriage are printed on the back of the ticket. Each ticket consists of several coupons which contain details of the flight:

- Audit-Coupon: copy for the accounts department
- Agent-Coupon: copy for the travel agent
- Flight-Coupons: copies for check-in procedures at the airport
- Passenger-Coupon: copy for the passenger

*1*

**Look at the ticket cover.**

1. The IATA was founded in 1945 as a voluntary association of scheduled air services.
   Do you remember what the abbreviation *IATA* stands for?
2. What is the difference between *scheduled flights* and *charter flights*?
   Make definitions using the prompts below:
   regular flights/occasional flights/organized by the company that owns the aircraft/usually offered in combination with package tours arranged by the tour operator

*2*

**On the ticket cover you find the term *baggage check*.**

1. What does it mean?
2. Which kinds of baggage (AE)/luggage (BE) do you have and what other pieces of baggage do people take on tour?

*3*

**Name the main functions of an airline ticket.**

# Unit 4

This is the inside of an IATA-ticket.

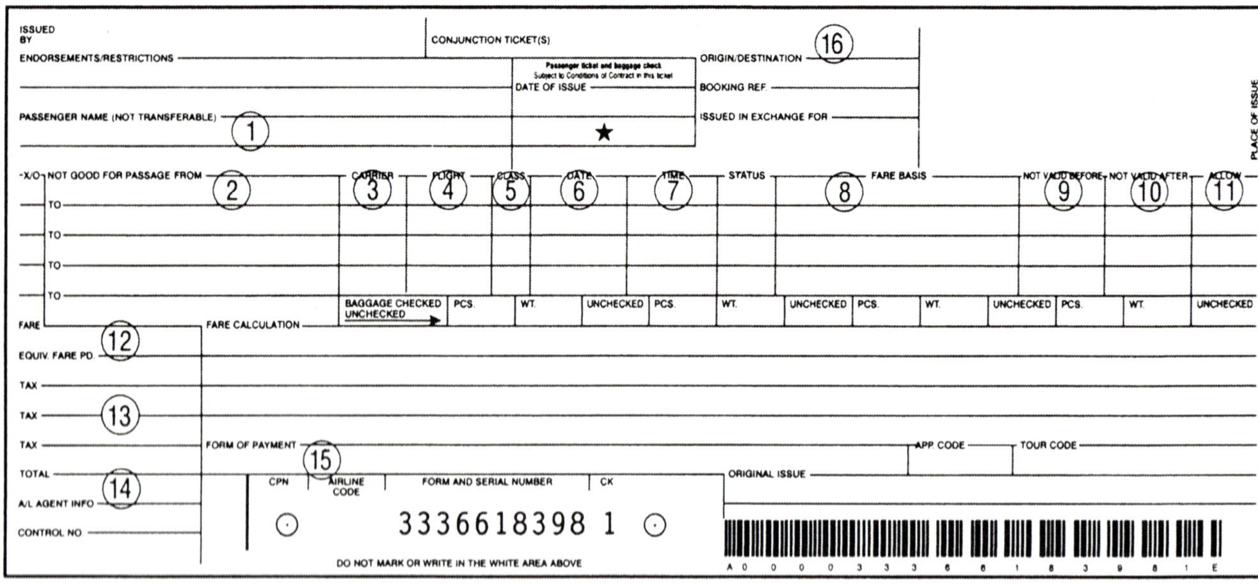


4 **Do you know what has to be filled** in the areas indicated by the numbers? Match the letters accordingly.

a) latest return date
b) indicators for first, business or economy class
c) passenger's itinerary
d) method of payment
e) basis for price calculation
f) traveller's first and family name
g) taxes, fees or charges
h) final price
i) flight number
j) place of departure, place of arrival
k) free baggage allowance
l) scheduled date of departure
m) 2-letter-airline code
n) earliest departure date
o) local departure time
p) price

In the meantime Teresa's ticket has been issued. Now she wants to collect it.

5 **Prepare to explain the ticket in full detail to the class.** Start like this:
*This is your ticket. It is issued by ... . You will leave from ... on ... . (...)*

The travel agent explains to Teresa that if she cancels the flights a cancellation charge has to be paid. If she wants to rebook the flights, she has to pay an amendment charge.



505226

## 4.4 At the airport

Have a look at these information boards.

**Departures** 17:30

| Scheduled | Flight Number | | To | Gate | Expected | Remarks |
|---|---|---|---|---|---|---|
| 17:45 | AC | 1371 | London | 102 | | boarding |
| 17:50 | LH | 6841 | Frankfurt | 113 | 18:20 | delayed |
| 18:00 | SU | 302 | Moscow | 99 | | boarding |
| 18:05 | AA | 6760 | Miami | 95 | | check in |
| 18:10 | AZ | 6657 | Palermo | 111 | 18:45 | delayed |
| 18:15 | SR | 135 | Zurich | 107 | | |
| 18:30 | CX | 829 | Hong Kong | | | |

**Arrivals** 17:30

| Scheduled | Flight Number | | From | Gate | Expected | Remarks |
|---|---|---|---|---|---|---|
| 17:35 | AZ | 650 | Rome | 63 | 17:30 | landed |
| 17:40 | AV | 020 | Bogota | 67 | | |
| 18:00 | CP | 6348 | Chicago | 52 | | |
| 18:15 | BA | 4451 | London | 68 | 20:00 | delayed |
| 18:30 | UA | 3261 | New York | 58 | | |
| 18:35 | KL | 691 | Amsterdam | 65 | | |
| 18:40 | QF | 512 | Sydney | | | |

For announcements of departures and arrivals the following prepositions are used:

| **Prepositions** | **Example** |
|---|---|
| of time | 1. Flight no. SU 114 leaves *at* 12.20 a.m.<br>2. Flight no. MS 6727 arrives *at* 16.05.<br>3. Flight no. LH 2413 arrives *in* 20 minutes. |
| of place | 1. Flight no. SU 114 to Moscow leaves *from* gate B 14.<br>2. Flight no. MS 6727 from Cairo arrives *at* gate B 18.<br>**Notice:**<br>Flight no. LH 6401 arrives <u>*at*</u> Frankfurt airport.<br>**but:**<br>Flight no. LH 6401 arrives <u>*in*</u> Frankfurt. |
| other uses | Flight no. SU 610 is *on time*. |

*1* **Take turns in asking for/giving information about the flights** shown on the information boards above. Use the prepositions from the box.

**2** **What's the opposite?**

1. arrival
2. take-off
3. domestic flight
4. to miss a plane
5. to be delayed
6. origin

## Giving directions

Teresa has arrived at Toronto International Airport.

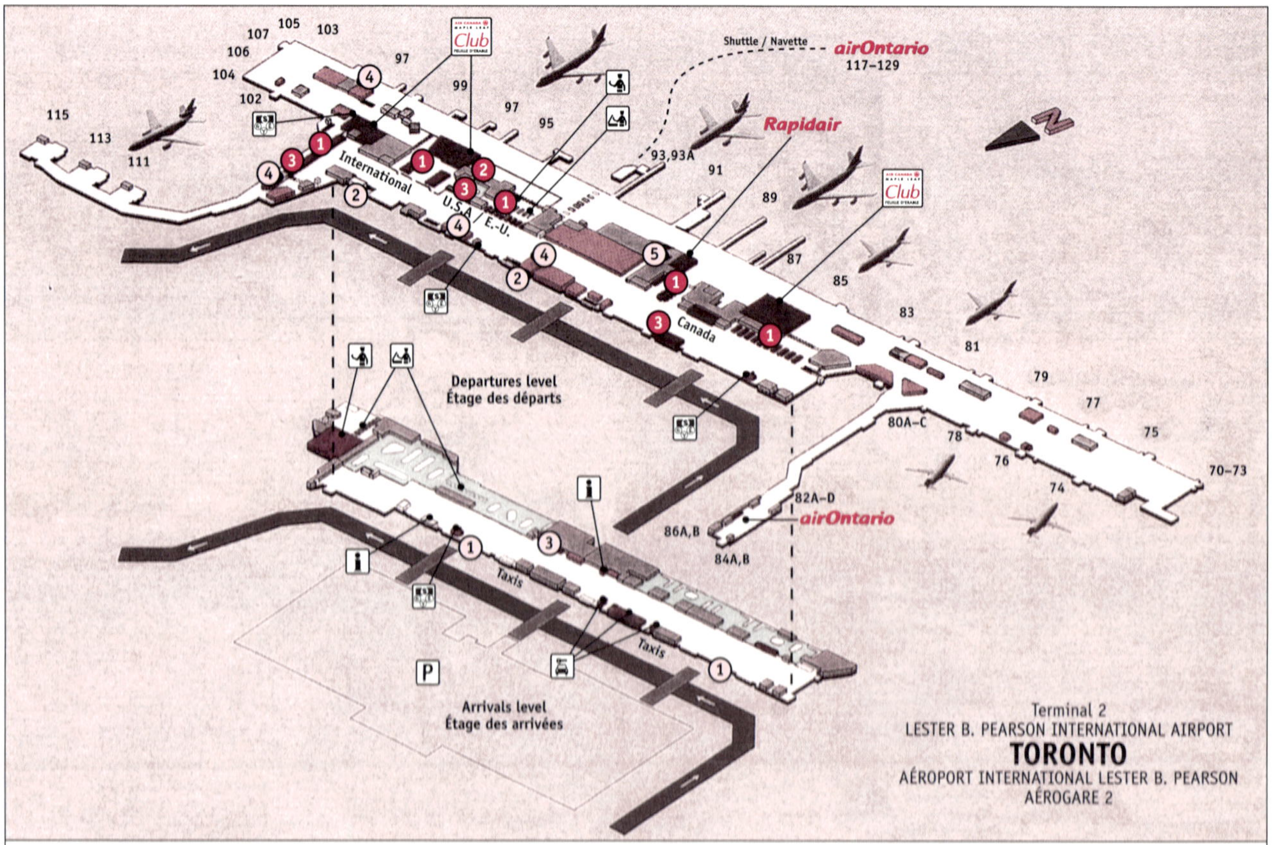


### KEY / LÉGENDE

- Club: Maple Leaf Lounge, Xerox Business Centre / Salon Feuille d'érable, Centre de bureautique Xerox
- Rapidair: Lounge / Salon
- ❶ Check-in counter / Comptoir d'enregistrement
- ❷ Connecting flights counter / Comptoir – correspondances
- ❸ Air Canada Special Services counter / Comptoir – services spéciaux Air Canada
- ① Shuttle service (city and hotels) / Service de navettes (ville et hôtels)
- ② Shuttle service (other terminals) / Service de navettes (autres aérogares)
- ③ Baggage storage / Consigne
- ④ Duty-free shops / Boutiques hors taxes
- ⑤ Play area for children / Aire de jeu pour enfants
- Restaurants, shopping / Restaurants, boutiques
- Baggage claim area / Retrait des bagages
- Information / Renseignements
- Car rental / Location de voitures
- Customs / Douane
- Bank or currency exchange office / Banque ou bureau de change
- Connecting flights / Vols de correspondance
- Immigration
- P Parking / Stationnement

First, she goes to the nearest information counter and asks where her connecting flight leaves from. The clerk sends her to the connecting flights counter (❷) which is upstairs on the departures level. Her flight leaves from gate 97.

As she has plenty of time left she decides to do some duty-free shopping (④). Then Teresa has a coffee in the restaurant near the children's play area (⑤).

Before she goes back to gate 97 she wants to change some money. Unfortunately, the first money exchange office is closed; so she has to go all the way down to the other end of the terminal.

Finally, Teresa goes to the nearest international check-in counter (❶) where she is planning to meet her friend Paul from Toronto.



505228

3

**Now, trace her steps.** Describe the way through the airport with the help of this substitution table:

| | | | | | |
|---|---|---|---|---|---|
| Teresa | goes straight | down<br>along | this hall<br>this way | as far as<br>to<br>past | the duty-free shop.<br>...<br>... |
| Teresa | takes the | first<br>second<br>... | turning on the | left.<br>right. | |
| Teresa | turns | left<br>right<br>around | at<br>behind<br>in front of | the money exchange office.<br>...<br>... | |

## At the check-in counter

This is Paul Smith from Toronto.

4

**What do you know about Toronto?**

1. Toronto is the capital of the state of
   a) Sasketchewan.
   b) Ontario.
   c) Québec.
2. In the picture you can see the
   a) Sears Tower.
   b) Empire State Building.
   c) CN Tower.
3. Toronto is located at
   a) Lake Placid.
   b) Lake Erie.
   c) Lake Ontario.

**5** **Complete the following dialogue** between Paul and the airline assistant with suitable words from the list below.

*Airline assistant:* Good evening, sir.

*Paul:* Good evening.

*Airline assistant:* May I have your ticket and passport, please?

*Paul:* Here you are.

*Airline assistant:* Thank you. – How many pieces of (1) do you have?

*Paul:* Just one.

*Airline assistant:* Could you please put it on the (2)?

*Paul:* Sure. Here you are.

*Airline assistant:* Oh, it's six pounds over.

*Paul:* Are your sure it's (3)?

*Airline assistant:* I'm afraid it is.

*Paul:* Do I have to pay an (4)?

*Airline assistant:* No, it's OK.

*Paul:* How nice! Would you like to join Teresa and me for a drink in the (5) lounge then?

*Airline assistant:* (giggle) No, I'm afraid I'm on duty.

*Paul:* May I sit in the (6)?

*Airline assistant:* I'm sorry. It is a non-smoking flight. Would you like a (7)?

*Paul:* No, I'd prefer an (8) next to Teresa Burns, please.

*Airline assistant:* All right. This is your (9). Boarding time is 19.30. Please proceed to (10) 97. Then you can take a seat in the (11) until your flight is called.

*Paul:* Thanks very much.

*Airline assistant:* You're welcome. Have a nice trip.

| | | |
|---|---|---|
| single flight | excess baggage charge | window seat |
| luggage | package holidays | carrier |
| scales | amendment charge | aisle seat |
| minimum connecting time | VIP | boarding pass |
| destination | fare | booking reference |
| overweight | smoking section | gate |
| scheduled flight | stand-by passenger | lounge |



505230

# 5.1 Staying in New York City

Sean and Una McPherson from the Republic of Ireland are planning to spend their honeymoon in New York City, because this has been highly recommended by their travel agent.

**1** **Read what the travel agent told them** and decide whether he should be fired or not.

## *Tourist information about New York City*

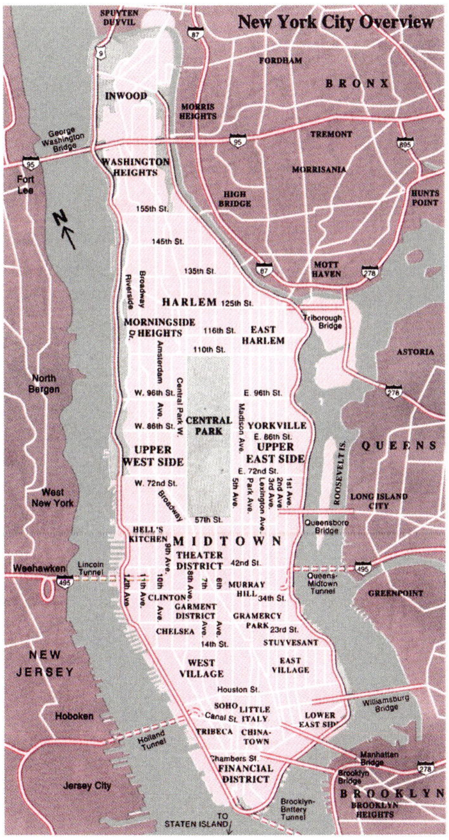


New York City's nickname is The Windy City. Arriving by boat you will pass The Victory Column and see the skyline dominated by the tower of the Empire State Building.

Having arrived, a modern public transport system of buses and subways takes you everywhere you like, but it is more convenient to stop one of the old black taxis which are typical for this city.

New York City has a lot of museums as well. One of the most famous is the Smithsonian with its unique architecture which is located on 5th Avenue. Just across the street is Hyde Park where you can do some roller skating, cycling or you simply relax.

5th Avenue is also famous for a lot of second hand shops. If you are lucky, you can find a new outfit in which you will be properly dressed for a theatre premiere on Wall Street.

New York City offers a large variety of food: Italian food, for example, is best served in Chelsea whereas you can get the best Chinese food in Hell's Kitchen.

**2** **Work in groups.** Collect as many pictures of and information on New York City and its sights as possible. Make a collage and explain it to your classmates.

Cross-check the information in the text above with what you have found out about the city.

## 5.2 Choosing the right accommodation

If you know someone who knows someone who lives in New York City – get that person's telephone number. Living in New York City is very expensive. At true full-service establishments, a night will cost you around $125 plus the hefty 13.25 % hotel tax. However, many reasonable choices are available for under $60 a night; it depends on your priorities. The young and the outgoing may prefer a budget-style place crowded with students. Honeymooning couples will not.

*1*

**Work with a partner.**

1. Think of as many different kinds of accommodation as possible.
2. Study the extracts from a tourist guide below and organize them from the cheapest to the most expensive kind of accommodation.

**Mansfield Hotel**, 12 W. 44th St. at 5th Ave. A dignified establishment housed in a turn-of-the-century building with comfortable leather couches in the lobby and beautiful oak doors in the hallways. Rooms in process of renovation: new lightning, new paint, and sauna whirlpool. Get one of the fixed-up ones. A bar/restaurant is conveniently located in the lobby. Check out at noon. Singles, doubles, triples, quads. Large suites for five people. Reservations and one night's deposit required.

**Big Apple Hostel**, 109th W. 45th St. Centrally located, offering new beds in clean, comfortable, carpeted rooms. Passport required. Double bed with desk and small clean bathroom or dorm-style beds with shared bathroom. Lockers. Free coffee. Reservations recommended. Reception open daily 8 a.m. – 3 a.m.

**YMCA**, 138–46 Northern Blvd. in Flushing Queens. Subway # 7 to Main St.; the YMCA is two blocks down. About 1/2 hr. from Manhattan. Men only. Gym, squash, and swimming facilities. 28-day maximum stay. Key deposit $ 20. Passport or driver's license required.

**The Waldorf-Astoria**, 301 Park Avenue. The passage of time has deepened the grace and elegance of this landmark Art Deco treasure. A privileged environment of eminent elegance, replete with unparalleled luxury and impeccable service. This is the exclusive hotel experience to indulge the most discriminating of travelers. Luxury awaits in exquisitely appointed king and double guestrooms and in a selection of suites. There is no charge for children, 18 and under, when they occupy the same room as their parents or grandparents. Make reservations online at www.waldorf-nyc.com, or call your professional travel agent, 1.800.HILTONS or The Waldorf-Astoria at 1.800.WALDORF. Outside the U. S., call Hilton Reservations Worldwide in your area.

*2*

**What do you expect of a full-service establishment?** Copy the following cluster into your notebook and complete it with your ideas.

Mr and Mrs McPherson would particularly like to stay at The Waldorf-Astoria from 2nd May to 9th May 20.. .
They have sent a letter to the hotel in which they enquire about:

- rooms & rates
- breakfast & dining options
- services & further facilities

**3** **You are a member of the Waldorf-Astoria staff.** Answer the McPherson's enquiry.

Write your offer according to the substitution table and the model letter in the appendix to:

Sean and Una McPherson, 10, The Pines, Brierfield, Castletroy, Limerick, Ireland.

Use the information given in this Waldorf-Astoria leaflet.

## GUEST ROOMS

*RATES ARE BASED ON SINGLE OCCUPANCY, PER NIGHT*

| | January 1 - June 27 |
|---|---|
| **DELUXE** | **$295 - 459** |

Accommodations include choice of King or Double-Double bedded rooms. Add an additional $40.00 per person, per night. Maximum 4 adults. There is no charge for children 18 and under when they occupy the same room as their parents or grandparents.

*Add $40 per room, per night to upgrade to the Executive Level. Enjoy expanded continental breakfast, hors d'oeuvres, desserts, afternoon tea and non-alcoholic beverages in the relaxing atmosphere of the Executive Lounge. Cocktails are available for purchase through our Honor Bar.*

## SUITES

*RATES ARE PER SUITE, PER NIGHT*

| | January 1 - June 27 |
|---|---|
| **DIAMOND MINI SUITES** | **$305 - 675** |
| **SUTTON SUITES** | **$325 - 695** |
| **ASTOR SUITES** | **$385 - 755** |
| **LANDMARK SUITES** | **$395 - 865** |

All rates subject to 13.25% New York City/State tax plus an occupancy tax of $2.00 per room, per night. All rates quoted in US dollars, subject to availability and to change without notice. All major credit cards accepted.

*Ask About Our Weekend Packages*

- Impeccably designed guest rooms and a myriad of distinguished suites.
- Concierge and multi-lingual staff.
- ***Executive Level*** features upgraded room accommodations, and the exclusive benefits of our ***Executive Lounge***. Enjoy expanded continental breakfast, hors d'oeuvres, desserts, afternoon tea and non-alcoholic beverages. Cocktails are available through our Honor Bar.
- Access to Bloomberg Terminal for on-line financial information.
- DINING OPTIONS

  ***Peacock Alley*** for innovative French cuisine.

  ***Bull & Bear*** for steaks, chops and seafood.

  ***Inagiku*** for "NewStyle" Japanese cuisine.

  ***Oscar's*** for contemporary American Bistro cuisine.

  ***Cocktail Terrace*** for traditional afternoon tea and cocktails; live piano music featured nightly.
- COCKTAILS

  ***Peacock Alley Lounge,*** the place to see and be seen.

  A distinctive club-like atmosphere at ***Sir Harry's***.

  Celebrated mahogany ***Bar at Bull & Bear***.

  ***Oscar's Bar***, a convivial experience.
- *24-hour* ***Room Service***.
- 24-hour full service ***Business Center***.
- 3,000 square foot state-of-the-art ***Plus One Fitness Center***.
- Dual line speaker phones, modem hook-up and voice mail, in-room fax machine/printer/copier.
- ***On Command Video*** features newly released movie selections, video account status and check-out.
- 25 distinctive conference, convention and banquet facilities.
- Home to ***Kenneth's Hair Salon*** and other fashionable boutiques.

## 5.3 Food and lodging

Most hotels offer different categories of catering, i.e. they provide a large range of food and drink for their guests.

**1** **Copy the table into your notebook** and complete the following tasks.

| meals / lodging & food | breakfast | lunch | dinner |
|---|---|---|---|
| **bed & breakfast (B&B)** | ? | ? | ? |
| **half board** | ? | ? | ? |
| **full board** | ? | ? | ? |

1. Mark the meals that are included in the different categories of lodging and food.
2. Explain the difference between:
   - lunch & dinner
   - continental & English breakfast
   - dish & meal
   - jam & marmalade

   You may look up the definitions in an English-English dictionary.
3. Decide which of the following things British or American people would prefer for breakfast:

   sausages, French toast, toast & marmalade, bacon & eggs, muffins, baked beans, peanut butter, fried mushrooms, a mug of coffee, orange juice, cereals, scrambled eggs, a cup of tea, fried eggs sunny side up, pancakes & maple syrup

## A candlelight dinner at the Waldorf-Astoria Bull & Bear

In the meantime the McPhersons have arrived at the Waldorf-Astoria. They want to start their honeymoon with a romantic dinner by candlelight.

### *Candlelight Menu*

| | |
|---|---|
| *Starters* | ***Soup of the Day***<br>***Shrimp Cocktail*** |
| *Main Course* | ***Roasted Filet of Lamb with Ratatouille, Rosemary Sauce***<br>***Roasted Salmon over Fennel & Celery Root with Tarragon Cream Sauce***<br>***Crispy Polenta***<br>***The Classic Caesar*** |
| *Desserts* | ***Orange Cream***<br>***Panna Cotta*** |

*Reception waiter:* Good evening, madam. Good evening, sir.

*Mr McPherson:* My name is McPherson. We've booked a table for two for nine o'clock.

*Reception waiter:* Ah, Mrs and Mr McPherson. Would you come this way, please?

*Mr McPherson:* Thank you.

***



505234

*Waiter:* Would you like an aperitif before you order?
*Mr McPherson:* No, I think we'd like to order straight away.
*Waiter:* I'd recommend our Candlelight Menu.
*Mr and Mrs McPherson:* Thank you. Let's see ...

***

*Waiter:* Have you decided yet?
*Mrs McPherson:* My husband would like to have the lamb and I'll go for the salmon for the main course.
*Waiter:* And to start with?
*Mrs McPherson:* The soup of the day for my husband and the shrimp cocktail for me, please.
*Waiter:* Have you decided on side dishes yet?
*Mr McPherson:* Oh yes, the crispy polenta for me, please. What about you, dear?
*Mrs McPherson:* No thanks, I'm fine.
*Waiter:* Would you like some white wine then?
*Mr McPherson:* What about a bottle of Chablis to start with, Una?
*Mrs McPherson:* Yes, that's alright with me, but I'd also like to have some sparkling water.
*Waiter:* Very good, thank you.

***

*Waiter:* Did you enjoy your meal?
*Mr and Mrs McPherson:* Oh yes, it was perfect.
*Waiter:* Would you like some coffee or dessert now?
*Mr McPherson:* Can you recommend anything?
*Waiter:* Sure, the orange cream is delicious.
*Mrs McPherson:* That sounds interesting. I'll try that.
*Mr McPherson:* For me just a cup of coffee, please. I don't want any dessert.

***

*Waiter:* Is everything alright?
*Mr McPherson:* Yes, may I have the bill, please?
*Waiter:* I can also put it on your room number.
*Mr McPherson:* Oh yeah, that's even better.

***

*Mrs McPherson:* Darling, don't forget to leave some tip for him.

**2** **Find headlines for the different steps of the conversation** between the McPhersons and the waiter.

**3** **Study the table below.** Now reread the dialogue and make a list of all countable and uncountable nouns as indicated by the examples.

| Nouns | Used for | Example |
|---|---|---|
| countable | things that can be counted.<br>They can be singular or plural. | I eat *a banana* every day.<br>I like *bananas*. |
| uncountable | things that cannot be counted.<br>They have only one form. | I eat *rice* every day.<br>I like *rice*.<br>**but:** *a bowl of* rice,<br>*two bowls of* rice. |

**4** **Study this table now** and explain the use of *some* and *any* in the dialogue above.

| | Used for | Example |
|---|---|---|
| some | positive sentences.<br>questions, when things are offered or asked for. | He ordered *some* salad.<br>Would you like *something* to eat?<br>Can I have *some* sugar, please? |
| any | negative sentences.<br>in most questions. | He did *not* order *any* salad.<br>Do you have *any* ice creams? |

**5** **Eating out: dream or disaster?**

What can go wrong while dining at a restaurant? Write a short story about it.

## 5.4 At the reception: telephoning

These are phrases that are commonly used in telephone conversations.

I'll just check that (for you).
Can I be of any assistance?
One moment, please. I'll put you through.
I'm sorry, the line is engaged.
Could you repeat that, please?
Goodbye.
Could I have your name, please?
I'll try again later.
Hello. This is ...
Would you like to speak to ... (instead)?
Reservations. Can I help you?
If you give me your number/name, I'll ask him to call you back.
Thank you for your help.
I'm afraid he isn't in at the moment.
Could you spell that, please? (Check appendix for word spelling alphabet!)
OK. I'll hold the line.
Can I take a message?
Thanks for calling. Goodbye.
I'm sorry, there is no answer from room no. 301.
I'm afraid the line is busy at the moment.
May I talk/speak to ..., please?

*1*

**Read the callouts.** Which of the phrases are useful for the following situations?
- opening the phone call
- saying that someone is not available
- connecting somebody
- the line is engaged
- ending the phone call

Copy them accordingly into your notebooks.

*2*

**Make up telephone dialogues** for the following settings or any other you like:

| **Setting 1: Booking a room** | |
|---|---|
| **Caller** | **Receptionist/ Reservations Clerk** |
| You want to book a room for your family (yourself, wife/husband, one child aged 7) at the Waldorf-Astoria. Ask for: categories of rooms, rates, availability. | Put caller through to reservations. Offer a double or twin-bedded room plus extra bed, a 3-bed room or suite, quote rates, decide on availability. |

| **Setting 2: Complaining** | |
|---|---|
| **Caller** | **Receptionist** |
| You have room no. 407 at the Bates' Motel. Call reception and complain about: no towels in private bathroom, chambermaid hasn't turned up yet, sheets are dirty, ants are constructing major road through mini-bar. | Tell caller that chambermaid is on holiday, ask if caller wants to talk to manager (if so, tell caller that manager will call back as soon as possible), send room service to rescue the last bar of chocolate from ants. |

*3*

**Explain the following words and expressions in English:**
- receiver
- yellow pages
- directory
- to be cut off
- to dial
- to hang up
- area code
- operator



505236

## 6.1 At the station

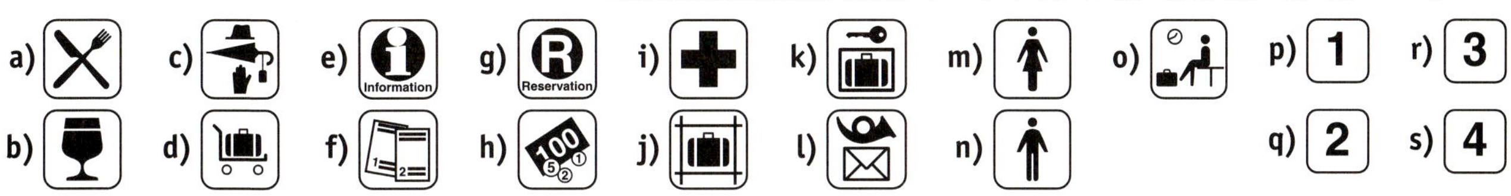


**1** **Match the station vocabulary with the pictograms and numbers.**

information counter/office, luggage (BE)/baggage (AE) trolley, lost and found counter/office, timetable (BE)/schedule (AE), platform, porter (BE)/baggage handler (AE), left-luggage office (BE)/baggage check room (AE), passenger's (BE)/traveler's (AE) aid, ladies' toilet, gents' toilet, left-luggage lockers, exchange office, rails (BE)/track (AE), waiting room, restaurant, ticket office, post office, booking office, buffet

**2** **Study this table and make sentences using the genitive** with the words below according to the examples.

a) porter/trolley
b) information counter/office hours
c) dog/leash
d) children/luggage
e) the Martins/train tickets
f) station/clock

| Genitive | Used for | Example |
|---|---|---|
| ~'s | people or animals.<br>**but:** after plural nouns ending in "s" we put ~' only | The *traveler's* aid is closed.<br>The *bird's* cage is open.<br>The *gents'* toilet is blocked. |
| of | things. | The name *of the restaurant* is 'The Cockroach'. |

# 6.2 Touring Britain by train

## *Railways in Britain*

The first regular passenger railway opened in 1830 between Liverpool and Manchester. At first, there were lots of private railway companies – at one time as many as 250 – which had their own lines and stations. Each company also had a terminus in London. The different termini still exist and are linked by the underground system.

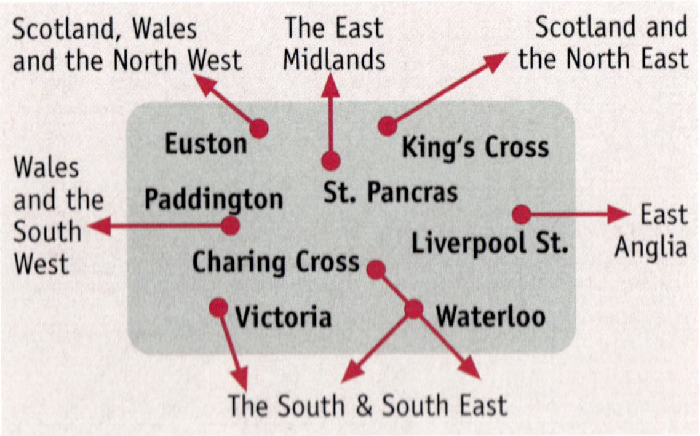


After the Second World War the government took over the different railway companies, which had already been reduced to four by 1921, and made them into one organisation – later called British Rail.

Since 1995 a process of privatisation has taken place again throughout the railways in Britain. There are now 25 train-operating companies, each of which is responsible for the services on individual lines. BritRail products provide one simple point of access to them all. BritRail tickets can be used on trains operated by any of the different companies all over Britain.

There is no need to buy separate tickets – with BritRail tickets and passes, the freedom to travel is yours.

*1*

**Complete these tasks about railways in Britain.**

1. What is the difference between a *station* and a *terminus?*
2. Explain why there are so many different termini in London.
3. Discuss the advantages and disadvantages of the privatisation of the railway system.

In the United States Mick and Mark Buchanan, twins from Memphis, Tennessee enquire about the BritRail Pass.

*2*

**Study the following information material** and explain to Mick and Mark how the BritRail Pass works.

Give information on:

- validity & prices
- age limit
- countries to be visited
- where to get the pass
- transfer service
- class of carriage

## *Information material about the BritRail Classic Pass Youth*

For those under 26 years of age we offer a terrific pass, a discounted version of the BritRail Classic Pass, which provides unlimited access to the entire rail network in England, Scotland and Wales at a splendid price.

***You get:***

★ Four consecutive day pass durations to choose from: either 8, 15 or 22 days or one month unlimited travel

★ Heathrow Express rail service between London Heathrow Airport and Paddington Station (constitutes a day travel on your pass)

★ Gatwick Express rail service between London Gatwick Airport and Victoria Station (constitutes a day travel on your pass)

★ 2nd class train travel

| *Prices* | *Youth 2nd class* |
|---|---|
| 8 days | $215.00 |
| 15 days | $280.00 |
| 22 days | $355.00 |
| 1 month | $420.00 |

**Please note:** Youth fare available only for passengers under 26 on their first date of travel. Prices are in US dollars and are subject to change. BritRail Passes cannot be purchased in Britain.



505238

Globetrotters Mick and Mark arrived in London a couple of days ago.

3 **Have you ever been to London?**

1. Which sights of London are shown above?
2. What other tourist attractions are there?

4 **After spending some time in London** Mick and Mark decide to travel to some other famous places in Britain, too. Take a map of Great Britain. Pick a few places of interest and make up an itinerary for the twins.
Explain what to see and what to do there.

## *On the train*

The first car of a train is the engine and several coaches follow. Travellers can choose between first and second class. In both classes there are different ways of seating: compartment and open-plan seating. In a compartment up to six people can take their seats facing each other. In open-plan seating areas the seats are in rows, similar to those in planes. Some of the seats are arranged in groups with tables in the middle. Above the seats there is a luggage rack, where passengers can store their bags and suitcases. At the end of each coach you find a washroom and toilet.

Some travellers such as businessmen or mothers with small children have special requirements. For these passengers there are special facilities: conference compartments with all the office equipment a modern businessman needs and mother and child compartments offering all a modern mother requires.

Hungry travellers find refreshments in the restaurant or dining car. Passengers who travel overnight can spend a restful night in the sleeping car. For low-budget travellers couchette accommodation is a cheaper alternative to sleepers. Passengers spend the night in 4 or 6-berth compartments. These are not as comfortable as single or double-berth-sleeper compartments. Bulky luggage can be stored in the luggage van or baggage car, which is usually the last coach of the train.

5 **Read the text above and complete the tasks below.**

1. Copy the train-related vocabulary into your notebooks.
2. Find pros and cons for compartment and open-plan seating.
3. What will the business traveller find in a conference compartment?
4. What do you think are the facilities a modern mother requires?
5. Mick and Mark want to travel overnight. Would you rather recommend sleeping-car or couchette accommodation? Explain why.
6. Think of different kinds of luggage and decide whether they should be stored in the luggage rack or baggage car.

6 **As you know Mick and Mark are twins.** Think of any funny confusions caused by twins. Write a short story or role play about it. The setting is a train. Use at least ten of the words you copied into your notebooks.

## 6.3 Special trains

### *Travel Eurostar...*

... and you'll wonder why you ever went any other way.

To travel Eurostar is to travel in style: More civilised. More convenient. More relaxing. More how travel should be. Simple check-in. No long queues. No hike to a distant departure gate.

You go from city centre to city centre. London Waterloo International to Paris Gare du Nord in three hours or Brussels Midi/Zuid in just two hours and forty minutes. You get an uninterrupted journey that actually makes travel enjoyable again.

Settle into a generous seat that invites you to relax. Read a book, catch up on your e-mail, make a call or two on your mobile phone. Get up and stretch your legs. Or just sit back and watch the countryside whisper by.

*1*

**Complete these tasks on the Eurostar.**

1. Where do you think has this text been taken from? What makes you think so?
2. Make a list of all the adjectives that describe the way of travelling by Eurostar. What impression is created by them?
3. Explain the sentence 'Sit back and watch the countryside whisper by.'

*2*

**There are other ways of travelling from London to Paris or Brussels.**

Name them and compare their advantages and disadvantages to those of travelling by Eurostar.

*3*

**Now read the text on the famous** Orient-Express and write down key words for the most important steps in its history.

### *The Orient-Express*

The history of 'luxury' train travel can be traced back to 1864 when the innovative railway builder George Mortimer Pullman created a train in Britain, featuring the ultimate in nineteenth century technology and being far more advanced than anything that existed in Europe.

Georges Nagelmackers, a young Belgian railway enthusiast, also began building luxury railway carriages and gradually proceeded to do for continental train travel what Pullman had done for Britain: With sleeping carriages and restaurant cars in place, Nagelmackers was finally able to fulfill his dream and on 4 October 1883 the first Orient-Express train service was inaugurated. The initial route ran from Paris to Romania, via Strasbourg, Vienna, Budapest and Bucharest.

By the turn of the century, the great age of rail travel was in full swing. The Simplon Tunnel – at 20.125 kms, the world's longest – was built in 1906, cutting the trip from Paris to Venice significantly, and by 1921 the Orient-Express was running an extended Simplon-Orient-Express route to Istanbul.

The 1920s and 1930s were the heyday of the legendary train. The list of Orient-Express passengers read like a who's who of international royalty and celebrities. After World War II however, the fortunes of the Orient-Express declined with the onset of cheaper air travel and holiday packages. In 1977 the service was finally closed down.

In May 1982 the legend was reborn when the Venice Simplon-Orient-Express made its maiden run from London to Venice.

*4*

**Today the world of the Orient-Express** has expanded and passengers can now enjoy the unique experience in the Far East on board the 'Eastern & Oriental Express', in Australia on board the 'Great South Pacific Express', and even on a cruise ship in Burma on board the 'Road To Mandalay'.

Now it's your turn! Work in groups and prepare a presentation of one of the routes mentioned above.

- ☞ For information material check the internet or send an enquiry to the Venice Simplon-Orient-Express Ltd.
- ☞ Check the appendix for how to write an enquiry and how to give a presentation.

ORIENT-EXPRESS
TRAINS & CRUISES

## 7.1 Test the West

Thelma Ingram and Louise Carter from Sydney, Australia need a rest from work. They have always wanted to tour the west of the USA.

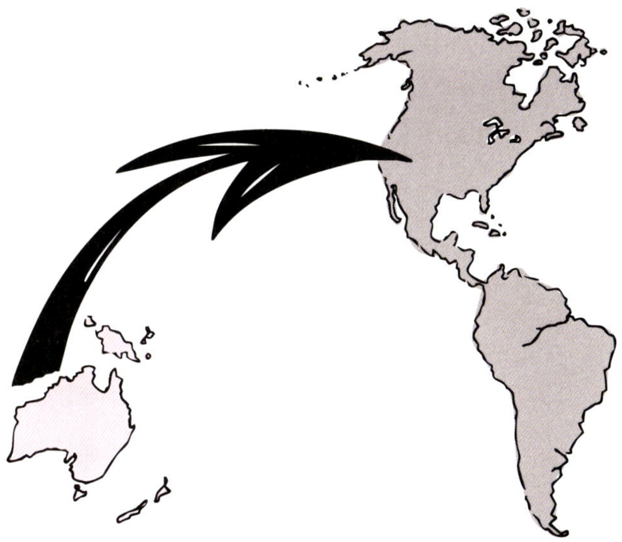

**1**

**Thelma and Louise have made a list of famous sights and places** they want to see.

1. Match the sights and places with their attractions and activities.

| | |
|---|---|
| 1. Disneyland | a) giant redwoods |
| 2. Yellowstone NP | b) egg-frying ground temperature of 200 °F |
| 3. San Diego | c) divorces |
| 4. Grand Canyon NP | d) Golden Gate Bridge |
| 5. Las Vegas | e) spiritual centre of the Mormons |
| 6. Death Valley NP | f) famous for film stars |
| 7. Hollywood | g) washed out by the Colorado River |
| 8. San Francisco | h) secret airbase (which isn't secret anymore) |
| 9. Area 51 | i) spouting geysers |
| 10. Yosemite NP | j) theme park |
| 11. Salt Lake City | k) world-famous zoo, Sea World |
| 12. Reno | l) gambling and instant marriages |

2. Decide whether the following statements are true or false.
   1. Silicon Valley is famous for breast implants.
   2. 'Cable car' is a synonym for 'electric car'.
   3. Mount Rushmore portrays four famous presidents of the USA.
   4. The Mount Rushmore National Monument is located in Hollywood.
3. Find the places and sights from exercises 1. and 2. on a map.

**2**

**If you wanted to go to the USA, what would you like to see?** Collect some photos, tell your classmates what to do and see there and try to convince them to travel with you.

## 7.2 Renting a car

Thelma and Louise have decided to travel by car. This is an application form of a car rental company in San Francisco.

ENROLLMENT FORM

**TO JOIN BUDGET EXPRESS/FASTBREAK AND PERFECT DRIVE, COMPLETE AND SIGN THIS MASTER RENTAL AGREEMENT ENROLLMENT FROM.** Once we receive this form from you, we'll give you a Perfect Drive membership number which you must use every time you rent in order to earn points.

First Name ______ Last Name ______

Street Address ______ City ______ State/Province ______

Zip/Postal Code ______ Country ______ Home Phone (    ) ______

Date of Birth (Month/Day/Year) ______ Driver's License No. ______

Issuing State/Province ______ Issuing Country ______ Expiration Date (Month/Day/Year) ______

**In order of preference, list up to 2 valid credit cards you wish to use for Budget rentals. At least one major card or Budget charge card must be provided to rent with the Budget Master Rental Agreement.**

Credit Card Type ______ Expiration Date (Month/Year) ______ Account Number ______

Credit Card Type ______ Expiration Date (Month/Year) ______ Account Number ______

**OPTIONAL PROTECTIONS:**

After reading the Budget Master Rental Agreement Terms and Conditions and the optional protection plan brochure, please select the optional protections you wish to purchase when using the Budget Master Rental Agreement. When you select an optional protection, you will be provided that optional protection where it is available.

**You must check Accept or Decline for each of these options:**

| | | | |
|---|---|---|---|
| LDW | Loss Damage Waiver | Accept ___ | Decline ___ |
| SLI | Supplemental Liability Insurance: | Accept ___ | Decline ___ |
| PAE | Personal Accidental and Effects Insurance: | Accept ___ | Decline ___ |

**Car Class Preference:** (choose one)

- ❒ Economy (Hyundai Accent or similar)
- ❒ Full Size 2-Door (Mercury Cougar or similar)
- ❒ Compact (Ford Escort or similar)
- ❒ Full Size 4-Door (Mercury Sable or similar)
- ❒ Intermediate (Ford Contour or similar)
- ❒ Luxury (Lincoln Town Car or similar)

**Other Preferences:** (optional)

❒ Non-Smoking Car: Check here to indicate your preference for a non-smoking car, subject to availability.

**As renter, I have read and agree with the Budget Master Rental Agreement Terms and Conditions and this Enrollment Form. I have read and understand the LDW notices and other notices in the Terms and Conditions and I waive any right to read and sign the notices at time of rental.**

SIGNATURE: ______

Required for the Budget Master Rental Agreement

DATE: ______

Budget

**Get out of the ordinary.™**

**1** **Thelma and Louise are not familiar with car rental terms.** Complete the exercises below in order to help them:

1. What is a membership number and what do you need it for?
2. The car classes offered above are a variety of saloon cars (BE)/sedans (AE). However, there are more car types, such as the hatchback and the estate car (BE)/station wagon (AE). Match the car types with the pictures below.

①

②

③



505242

**2** **Read the text about car insurances.** Suggest a suitable protection plan for the following situations and explain why:

1. What if someone breaks into the car and steals all their luggage while Thelma and Louise are doing some sightseeing?
2. What if someone steals the whole car while Thelma and Louise are having a coffee break?
3. What if Thelma runs over an award-winning poodle and its mistress suffers a nervous breakdown?

## *Insurances for the car rental industry*

In most countries a basic liability insurance, also called third-party insurance, is compulsory. This insurance, however, only provides a limited injury and death cover to anyone injured or killed in an accident. Therefore car rental firms strongly recommend that you select optional insurance plans which protect renters during the rental period:

**Loss Damage Waiver (LDW)** is an option that relieves renters of financial responsibilities if the car is damaged or stolen while under rental contract. If you decline LDW you may be responsible for up to the full fair market value of the car if it is damaged, vandalized or stolen during the rental. You may also be responsible for reimbursing the car rental company for the revenue lost by not being able to use the car while it is being repaired or not recovered due to theft (loss of use).

**Supplemental Liability Insurance (SLI)** is an excess automobile liability insurance that protects you and all authorized drivers of the rental vehicle against third-party bodily injury and property-damage claims.

**Personal Accident and Effects Insurance (PAE)** protects you and your passengers against accident, injury and loss of personal property. PAE provides renters and occupants of the rental vehicle with accidental death benefit and coverage for certain medical expenses resulting from an accident. In addition, PAE provides protection against loss of or damage to certain personal property of the renter and individuals travelling with the renter.

Thelma and Louise have sent the enrollment form to the Budget car rental company. They have applied for an economy class car from 2 September 20.. to 23 September 20.. including LDW and SLI.

**3** **Below you find a letter of confirmation from Budget to Thelma.** Unfortunately it is mixed up. Rewrite the letter in the correct order and in full layout.

| | |
|---|---|
| Budget<br>Enrollment Services<br>PO box 110899<br>Carrollton, TX 75011–9974<br>USA | Thelma Ingram<br>230 Cowart Street<br>Sydney<br>New South Wales<br>Australia 2020 |

We also provide an LDW and SLI for the rental period.

Yours sincerely,
Frank Granato

On arrival at San Francisco Airport please present your personal membership number 007 1234 and booking reference number 007 1234/001 at our car rental desk.

We would like to confirm your booking of a Hyundai Accent for the period of September 2, .. to September 23, ...

The total amount of $650.00 will be drawn from your credit card account VISA 4508 2310 1425 6035.

Dear Mrs. Ingram,

# 7.3 Travelling by coach

In August Thelma and Louise meet their friends Bob and Sally who have just returned from a holiday in the USA. The home-comers are full of enthusiasm, tell stories and show pictures of their eventful trip. During that evening it turns out that Bob and Sally toured the United States by coach.

*1*

**Read the text about the Greyhound bus system** and answer the following questions:

1. How old is the Greyhound company?
2. Why is it called Greyhound?
3. Which areas does Greyhound serve?
4. Why do you think the majority of passengers is either young or old?

## *The Greyhound bus system*

In 1914, Carl Eric Wickman, an immigrant from Vamhus, Sweden, founded the company that became today's Greyhound Lines, Inc., when he began transporting miners between the villages of Hibbing and Alice, Minnesota, for 15 cents one-way or 25 cents round-trip on his seven-seat Hupmobile.

In 1921, the first real intercity buses manufactured were dubbed 'the Greyhounds' because of their sleek design and grey paint. The 'running dog' became the company's trademark as it remains today. The company mascot is called 'Lady Greyhound'.

Today, Greyhound Lines, Inc. with headquarters in Dallas, Texas, is the nation's largest bus company and the only nationwide provider of bus transportation that links urban, suburban, small-town and rural America. In many areas Greyhound provides the only regularly scheduled transportation service for miles around. Greyhound offers the opportunity to travel between almost any location in North America with safety and convenience.

Greyhound serves over 2,400 destinations in the 48 contiguous United States, with additional limited services into Canada and Mexico, encompassing more than 18,000 daily departures. By comparison, fewer than half that many US locations are served by the airlines and Amtrak. The company's primary business is scheduled passenger service for intercity bus transportation, but it also provides charter bus service, package express delivery service, and food service at certain terminals.

The average bus age in Greyhound's active fleet of more than 2,000 buses is 6.5 years. A bus weighs from 19,000 to 20,000 kgs and has 43 or 47 seats, depending on the model. Almost a third of all Greyhound passengers are senior citizens and another quarter are under 25 years old.

*2*

**The Americruiser is one of the various Greyhound coaches.** Match the vocabulary with the numbers indicated in the picture.

| | | |
|---|---|---|
| a) seats | b) tire (AE) / tyre (BE) | c) parcel racks |
| d) driver | e) reading lights | f) baggage compartments |
| g) restroom (AE) / toilet (BE) | h) picture windows | i) engine |

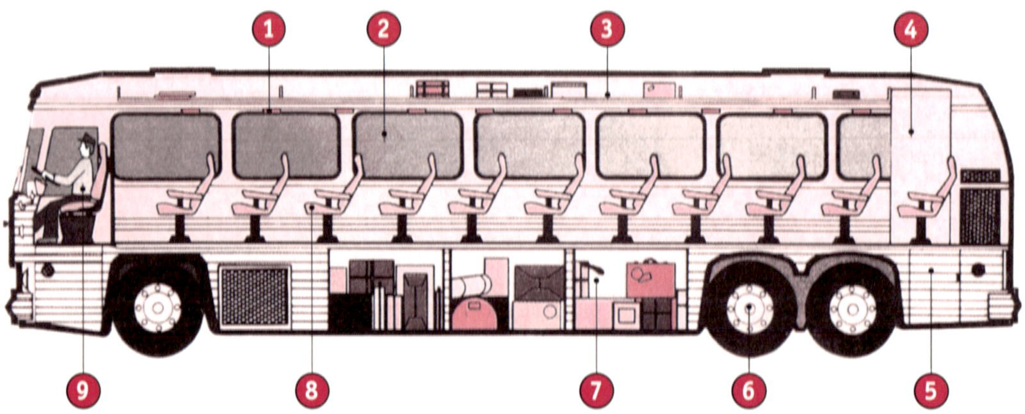

Adjectives and adverbs are used for descriptions.

| | Used for | Example |
|---|---|---|
| adjectives | description of nouns. | Tom is a *careful* coach driver. |
| adverbs | description of verbs<br>or<br>adjectives. | Tom drives the coach *carefully*.<br>Tom is an *extremely* good coach driver. |

You may have noticed that many adverbs are made from an adjective + **~ly**.

**but:** 1. Not all words ending in **~ly** are adverbs, e.g.: friendly, silly, lovely.

2. Not all adverbs end in **~ly**.

e.g.: good – *well* fast – *fast* late – *late* hard – *hard*

**Notice:** The adverb *hardly* does exist, but it has a completely different meaning:
He works *hard*. (= He works a lot.)
He *hardly* works. (= He works very little.)

**3** **Read the descriptions below** and transform the adjectives in parentheses into adverbs, if necessary.

a) The Americruiser has (special) seats, designed to give (firm) support and still be (comfortable). They are (full) (adjustable) so you can change positions as often as you like. Passengers have more space than on most other motor coaches.

b) You will never have a (bumpy) trip in a Greyhound Americruiser. You will travel (smooth) and (comfortable) instead, because of a (new) (developed) air-suspension system.

c) Inside, there are overhead parcel racks, so your carry-on luggage is (easy) (accessible).

d) An (experienced) driver treats you (courteous) during the trip.

e) (Individual) (controlled) reading lights are (easy) on your eyes.

f) (Roomy) baggage compartments guarantee that your group will not have to leave anything behind.

g) A (convenient) on-board restroom is provided.

h) (Extra-large) (tinted) picture windows, (double glazed) and (hermetical) sealed, allow a great view of the landscape.

i) The Americruiser runs (fuel-efficient) due to a (quiet) diesel engine. So you will be saving our natural resources while enjoying more miles for your money.

Thelma and Louise are quite impressed by the adventures Bob and Sally have told them. However, there are still some questions unanswered.

**4** **Find the suitable answer to Thelma's and Louise's questions.**

1. Is there assigned seating on Greyhound buses?
2. Are meals provided on board?
3. Is smoking allowed on buses?
4. Are stopovers permitted?
5. Are radios, laptops, cellular phones, or electronic games allowed on buses?
6. Are pillows and blankets available for night time travel?
7. Do the buses operate 24 hours a day?

a) Yes. Stopovers at any point along the route, within the limit of the ticket, will be permitted.

b) Radios, cellular phones or electronic games are allowed on buses, as long as they do not disturb fellow passengers and headphones are used.

c) No. Seating is on a first come, first served basis.

d) No, but you are welcome to bring your own within your carry-on luggage.

e) No. Meals are not provided, though there are regular meal stops on extended routes. Food and non-alcoholic drink may be carried on board for personal consumption.

f) No. Federal law does not permit smoking on Greyhound buses.

g) Yes. Greyhound buses travel around the clock, so you can travel by day and enjoy the scenery through wide panoramic windows. Or, select a night service, and relax in a reclining seat with reduced interior lighting.

## 8.2 On board the MS Patriot

The MS Patriot will take the Duckworths around the Hawaiian Islands.

**1**

**Study the various plans of the ship.**

1. Give information about technical data of the MS Patriot:
   - capacity & weight
   - length in feet and metres
2. 'A cruise ship is a floating five-star hotel.'
   a) Make a cluster of the facilities you expect to find on board.
   b) Study the ground plans of the Broadway and Bridge Deck and complete your cluster, if necessary.
3. Answer the following questions:
   a) Why is the Broadway Deck wider and longer than the Bridge Deck?
   b) What is the difference between a whirlpool and a wading pool?
   c) Is 'gift shop' a synonym for 'drugstore'?
   d) What kind of performances do you expect to find on the two different stages on Broadway Deck?
   e) What are the front and the back of a ship called?
   f) Where are the seven passenger elevators located?

**2**

**Have a closer look at the four different types of cabin accommodation!**

1. Decide whether the following statements are true or false.
   1. The Parlor Suite has approximately 152 sq. ft.
   2. The Interior Stateroom has a porthole window and a shower.
   3. The Superior Ocean View Stateroom may be twin-bedded.
   4. The Ocean View Stateroom has a shower and a bathtub.
2. Answer the following questions.
   a) What do you see when you look out of a porthole window?
   b) Is a picture window part of an Interior Stateroom that faces the photo gallery?
   c) Which one is more comfortable to sit in: a bathtub or a shower tub? Explain why.

**3**

**Work in pairs. Write a section for the MS Patriot cruise brochure.** Pick one of the headings below:

- Technical Data
- Facilities On Board
- Feeling At Home
- Enjoy yourself

For giving information the passive voice is frequently used to make the text more interesting.
Use the active and the passive voice in your section of the brochure.

| | Used for | Example |
|---|---|---|
| active | saying what the subject does. | The sailor *cleans* the deck. (object) |
| passive | saying what happens to the subject (= object of the active sentence). | The deck *is cleaned* (by the sailor). (subject) |
| | The passive is **be** (is/was/have been/etc.) + **past participle** (cleaned/built/etc.). | |



505248

**Broadway Deck**

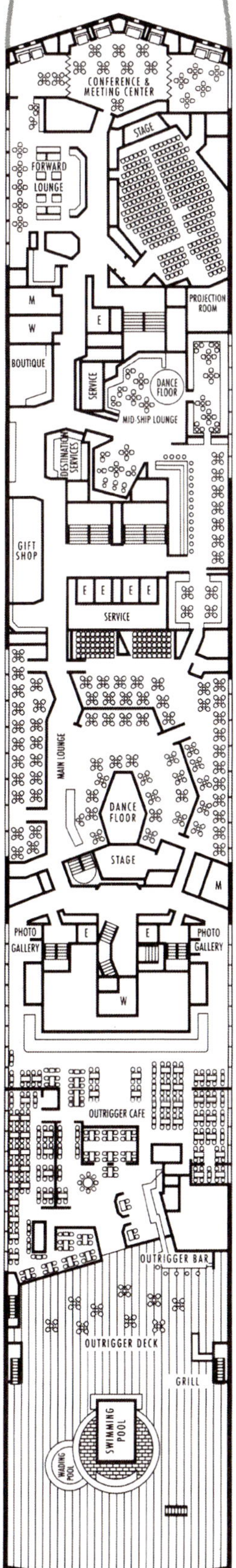


**Bridge Deck**
Rooms 050–091
184 ft from bow

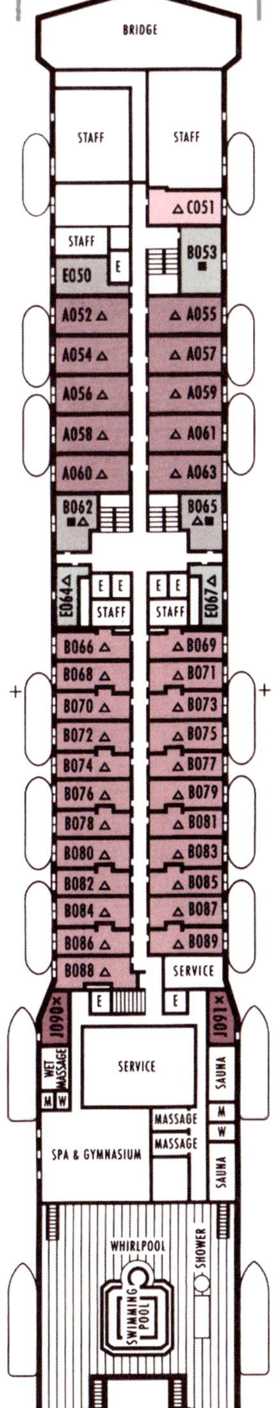


258 ft to stern from rooms 090 and 091

**Parlor Suite**
Approx. 294 sq. ft.
Features 1 king-size bed, 1 sofa bed, sitting area, picture window, refrigerator, bathtub and shower.
**A**

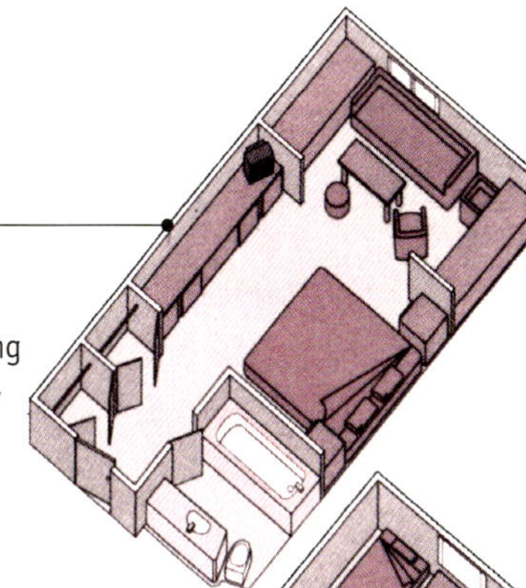

**Superior Ocean View Stateroom**
Approx. 219 sq. ft.
Features 2 lower beds or 1 queen-size bed, sitting area, window, bathtub and shower.
**B, C**

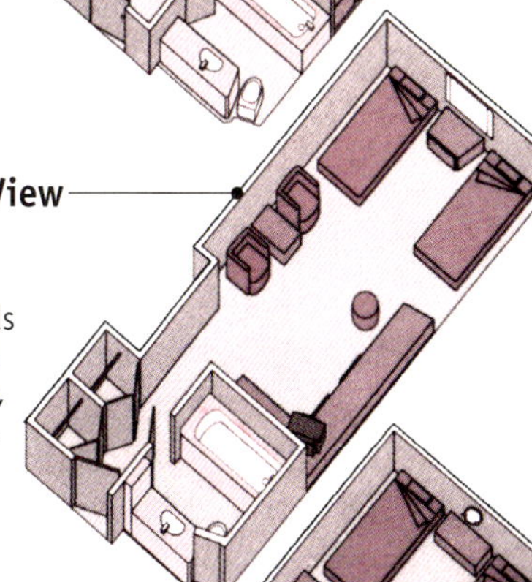

**Ocean View Stateroom**
Approx. 152 sq. ft.
Features 2 lower beds, or 1 queen-size bed, or 2 lower and 2 upper beds, porthole window and shower.
**D, E, F, G, H, I**

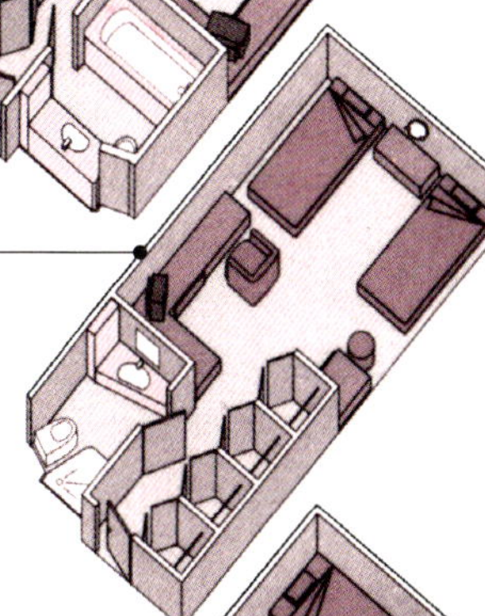

**Interior Stateroom**
Approx. 152 sq. ft.
Features 2 lower beds, or 1 queen-size bed, or 2 lower and 2 upper beds and shower.
**J, K, L, M, N**

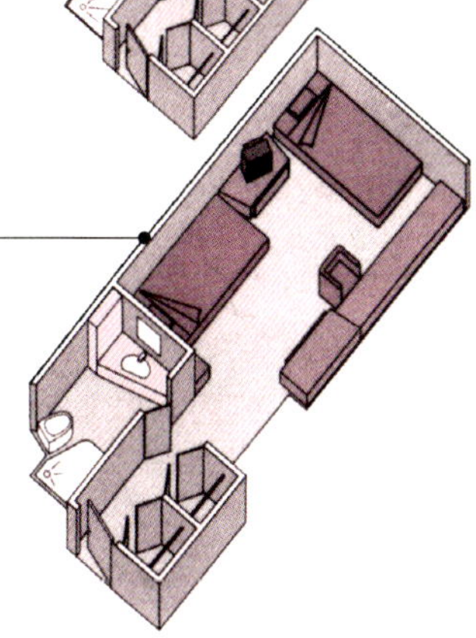

**Ship specifications & Facilities**

- 1,214 Passengers
- 33,930 gross tons
- 704 feet long
- Automatic Stabilizers
- 9 Passenger Decks
- 7 Passenger Elevators

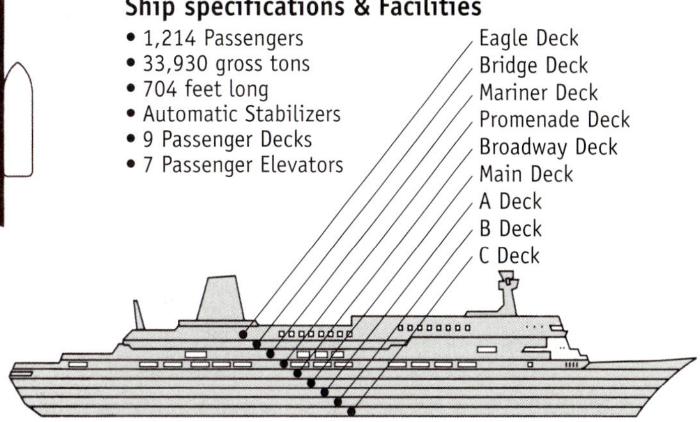


505249

## 8.3 Dealing with complaints

The Duckworths have enjoyed their cruise on the MS Patriot very much. Back at home they meet their neighbours, the Hardings, who have been on a cruise as well. They went on a seven-day tour around the Caribbean on the MS Challenge. This is what their holiday was like:

**1**

**Look at the pictures.**

1. What happened to the Hardings on board?
2. Who would you have complained to in the situations above? Explain why.
   - captain
   - chef
   - purser
3. Work in pairs. Take turns to be the purser and a guest of a cruise ship. Use the prompts below to make short dialogues. Try to use a different expression from the box to apologize each time.
   - no towels
   - noisy guest in next cabin
   - elevator does not work
   - bad cocktails
   - no drinks in mini bar
   - jellyfish in the pool

| Guest | Purser |
|---|---|
| I'd like to speak to the purser/manager/barkeeper/... | How can I be of assistance? |
| There is/are (no) ... | I'm (most) terribly/so sorry, sir/madam. |
| The... is/are not working/bad/too ... | I do apologize, ... |
| Thank you. | Please accept my/our apologies, ... |
| ... | I'll talk to ... |
| | I'll send ... |
| | I'll see to it that ... |
| | ... |

**2**

**The Hardings are not happy at all.** They spent $ 2,849 per person for their so-called 'holiday'. Write their letter of complaint in full layout to the tour operator.

Paradise Cruises Ltd., Calle Gertrudis # 8, 00911 San Juan, Puerto Rico

Ellen and Sam Harding, 3115 Pleasant Twp. Rd. 312 SE, Tampa, FL 43731

☞ Check the appendix for how to write a letter of complaint.

## Cruising the world

**3**

**Now it's your turn! Work in groups.** Pick one of the following destinations and prepare a presentation of available cruises.

- the Greater and Lesser Antilles
- the Mediterranean Sea
- the Nile

Give information about ports, excursions, shipping companies and their fleet.

☞ Check the appendix for how to give a presentation and how to write enquiries.

**4**

**Would you like to work on a cruise ship? Discuss.**

☞ Check the appendix for how to write an application.



505250

# The layout of a business letter

**Letterhead**

Sunshine Travels Ltd.
122 Brooklyn Avenue, Crooksville, OH 43731
USA

**Recipient's Address/Inside Address:**

UK: Rainbow Trekking Ltd.
135 Queen Street,
London W2P 5AG ← **Post Code**
ENGLAND

USA: Pacific Union Inc
Suite 12, Kennedy Building
267 Ocean Boulevard
Los Angeles, CA 10067 ← **ZIP Code** (Zone Improvement Plan)
USA

**Reference:**

our ref: invoice no. 32/00 Ba/Li

**Date:**

UK: 4 July 2001 *or* 4th July 2001
USA: July 4, 2001 *or* July 4th, 2001
ISO: 2001-07-04

**Attention Line**

Attention/Att./Attn.: Mr/Mrs/Ms (+ name)/Sales Manager

**Salutation**

UK: Dear Mr/Mrs/Ms (+ name), ← open punctuation = without full stop (.) in BE
Dear Sir(s)/Madam (Mesdames),
Dear Sir(s) or Madam (Mesdames),

USA: Dear Mr./Mrs./Ms. (+ name) ← closed punctuation = with full stop (.) in AE
Dear Sir(s) or Madam (Mesdames):
Gentlemen:/Ladies:
Ladies and Gentlemen:

**Subject Line**

enquiry, offer, confirmation, ...

**Body of the Letter**

**Complimentary Close**

UK: Yours sincerely,
Yours faithfully,

USA: Yours sincerely,/Sincerely yours,
Yours truly,/Truly yours,
Very truly yours,

**Signature Block**

Peter Smith ← If the letter is signed by someone other than the writer, **p.p.** *or* **per pro.** must be placed before the name (= Latin for *on behalf of*).
name printed
position

**Enclosure(s)**

Enc(s)/Encl

**Carbon Copy**

cc: Mr/Mrs/Ms (+ name)

# Enquiry (BE) / Inquiry (AE)

| | | | | | |
|---|---|---|---|---|---|
| I<br>We<br>My family (wife, child aged six) and I | intend<br>want<br>am/are planning | to | travel to<br>spend five weeks in | Mexico<br>South America<br>Australia<br>Indonesia | next summer. |

| | | | | |
|---|---|---|---|---|
| I<br>We | would like<br>want<br>wish | to know | about | geographic information.<br>general tourist information.<br>information about holiday resorts and local tours. |
| | am/are especially interested in | | | |

| | | | | | |
|---|---|---|---|---|---|
| Will<br>Would<br>Could | you | please<br>be so kind as to | send | me<br>us | some brochures?<br>some catalogues? |

| | | | | | |
|---|---|---|---|---|---|
| Particularly,<br>In particular,<br>For instance, | I<br>we | would | be grateful<br>be glad<br>like | to know more about | fares.<br>prices.<br>accommodation.<br>all-inclusive tours. |

| | | | | | |
|---|---|---|---|---|---|
| I<br>We | am/are looking forward to | hearing from you<br>receiving your reply | as soon as possible.<br>very soon.<br>in the near future.<br>in a few days time.<br>in due course. | | |
| | would | appreciate | receiving | an early<br>a prompt | reply. |
| | | be thankful<br>be grateful | for<br>to receive | | |

# Offer

| | | | | |
|---|---|---|---|---|
| Many thanks<br>Thank you | for your | enquiry<br>letter | of<br>dated | 5 September 2000. |

| | | |
|---|---|---|
| We | think you have made an excellent<br>appreciate your | choice. |

| | |
|---|---|
| We have the pleasure of | submitting the following offer.<br>offering you the following rooms. |

| | | | | | | |
|---|---|---|---|---|---|---|
| Our | establishment<br>hotel | has<br>offers | a wide | range<br>selection | of rooms and suites that will | appeal to you.<br>suit your needs.<br>meet your expectations. |

| | | | | | |
|---|---|---|---|---|---|
| All our rooms have | private bathrooms<br>air conditioning<br>telephone<br>... | and are | tastefully<br>luxuriously | furnished and fitted with | colour TV.<br>tea/coffee-making facilities.<br>... |



505252

| | |
|---|---|
| You can choose between<br>We can supply | full board.<br>half board.<br>bed & breakfast. |

**Please list rooms (e.g. single, double, etc.), rates/taxes and supplements.**

| | | | |
|---|---|---|---|
| For | leisure and health<br>your convenience | a swimming pool<br>sunbeds<br>a room service<br>… | is/are at your disposal. |

| | | | |
|---|---|---|---|
| Please find enclosed<br>As requested we are sending you | our | recent<br>latest | price list.<br>catalogue.<br>brochure. |

| | |
|---|---|
| We would like to thank you for | your interest.<br>writing to us. |

| | | | |
|---|---|---|---|
| If you have any<br>For | further questions don't hesitate to | contact<br>call<br>write to | us. |

## Confirmation

| | | |
|---|---|---|
| Thank your for your | letter<br>application form<br>enrollment form | of **(date)**. |

| | |
|---|---|
| We would like to confirm your booking of | a Hyundai Accent.<br>a double bedded room.<br>flight number … to **(destination)**. |

| | | | |
|---|---|---|---|
| The | price<br>fare | includes | LDW and SLI.<br>breakfast.<br>taxes. |

| | |
|---|---|
| The total amount of $ **(price)** will be | drawn from your account.<br>due on receipt of tickets. |

| | | | | |
|---|---|---|---|---|
| If | there is anything else I/we can do for you<br>you have any further questions | please do not hesitate to | get into touch<br>contact us | again. |

## Cancellation

| | | | | | | | |
|---|---|---|---|---|---|---|---|
| Unfortunately,<br>I am/We are sorry, but | | I<br>we | will not be able to travel | | | this year.<br>at that time.<br>in September. | |
| Owing to | illness<br>unforeseen circumstances | | may have to cancel | my<br>our | trip | | |
| | | | | | reservation<br>booking | for | this year.<br>that time.<br>September. |

| | |
|---|---|
| We would also like to know about<br>Could you inform me/us of | cancellation and/or amendment charges. |

| | | |
|---|---|---|
| I<br>We | grately appreciate<br>would like to thank you for | the time and trouble you took for me/us. |

## Complaint

| | | | | | |
|---|---|---|---|---|---|
| I<br>We | am/are sorry<br>regret having | to | tell<br>inform | you that your | ship cruise<br>Caribbean Cruise<br>package tour to **(destination)** |

| | | |
|---|---|---|
| from **(date)** to **(date)** has | not | met our expectations. |
| | | turned out to our satisfaction. |
| | given cause for complaint. | |

| | | |
|---|---|---|
| I am/We are writing to complain about the | way the staff treated me/us<br>service<br>meals | on board.<br>at the hotel. |
| | safety standards | of the ship.<br>of the hotel. |

**Please name reason(s) for complaint.**

| | | | | | | | |
|---|---|---|---|---|---|---|---|
| I/We tried to explain the | situation<br>problem | to the | purser<br>receptionist<br>manager | on duty but he was | extremely<br>very | rude<br>unfriendly | to me/us. |

| | | | | | | |
|---|---|---|---|---|---|---|
| I/We have | often<br>always | booked my/our | holidays<br>flights<br>accommodation | at your | company<br>agency<br>office | but if |

| | | | | |
|---|---|---|---|---|
| I/we do not receive a | satisfactory reply to this letter<br>considerable reduction in price<br>compensation | I/we will | take<br>do | my /our business elsewhere. |
| you do not settle this matter to our complete satisfaction | | | | |

| | | |
|---|---|---|
| I/We shall expect your | letter<br>reply | immediately.<br>by return of post. |

## Application

| | | | | | |
|---|---|---|---|---|---|
| With reference<br>In reply | to your advert in | yesterday's Travel Agent News<br>the Daily Mirror of **(date)**<br>the May edition of **(date)** | I | would like<br>wish | to apply for the |

| | | |
|---|---|---|
| job as | | **(job name according to ad)**. |
| position<br>post | of | |

| | | | |
|---|---|---|---|
| Since **(year/date)**<br>For the past ... years | I have been | a trainee<br>an apprentice | at **(name of company)** to become a travel agent. |

| | | | | | |
|---|---|---|---|---|---|
| During that time I have gained | | a good<br>a working<br>an expert | knowledge | of handling | CRS such as START/AMADEUS.<br>word-processing programmes.<br>counter and back-office work. |
| I am | experienced in<br>familiar with | | | | |

| | | | | | | | | | |
|---|---|---|---|---|---|---|---|---|---|
| I | specialized in | corporate travel<br>eco tourism | and I | have a | good<br>reading | knowledge<br>command | of | English<br>Spanish<br>Kiswahili | .<br>.<br>. |
| | speak | | | | | | | | fluently. |

| | | |
|---|---|---|
| I will | finish my apprenticeship<br>take my Chamber of Commerce exam | in **(year)**. |

| | | | |
|---|---|---|---|
| I am | applying for<br>particularly interested in | the job as **(name of job)**<br>this position | because **(reasons for applying)**. |

| | | | |
|---|---|---|---|
| Enclosed please find my | CV (BE)<br>curriculum vitae (BE)<br>résumé (AE) | and copies of | (school) certificates.<br>diplomas. |

## Résumé or CV

**Résumé**
(intended for an American reader)

Name:
Address:
Telephone:
Date of Birth:
Marital Status:
Nationality:

| | |
|---|---|
| Education | |
| years (from earliest to latest date) | Pupil at …<br>A-levels / Graduation from high school<br>Student of … |
| Employment | |
| years (from earliest to latest date) | Nanny for …<br>Practical training with …<br>Apprenticeship |
| Further Skills and Interests | Languages, …<br>Sports, … |
| References | |
| (if required) | Names, addresses and positions |

**Curriculum Vitae (CV)**
(intended for a British reader)

Name:
Address:
Telephone:
Date of Birth:
Marital Status:
Nationality:

| | |
|---|---|
| Education | |
| years (from latest to earliest date) | Student of …<br>A-levels / Graduation from high school<br>Pupil at … |
| Work Experience | |
| years (from latest to earliest date) | Apprenticeship<br>Practical training with …<br>Nanny for … |
| Skills | Languages, … |
| Personal interests | Sports, … |
| References | |
| (if required) | Names, addresses and positions |

## Giving a presentation

Possible sources of information:

- brochures/catalogues in your travel agency
- library/bookshop: guidebooks, maps, encyclopedias, dictionaries
- internet
- tourist boards

Possible media for giving a presentation:

- overhead projector, black board/white board, flip chart
- video, tape, slide projector
- posters, handouts, wall news-sheet
- role play, quizzes, games

Advice for presentations:

Keep in mind that the audience wants to be informed and entertained! Therefore:

- Greet the audience and give a short outline of your presentation.
- Support your presentation by using a variation of media to keep the audience's attention.
- Look for eye-to-eye contact with the audience.
- Speak slowly, clearly and loud enough.
- Never turn your back to the audience.
- Make short breaks to allow questions from the audience.
- Thank the audience for their attention.

## Word spelling alphabet

| | | | |
|---|---|---|---|
| **A**lfa | **H**otel | **O**scar | **V**ictor |
| **B**ravo | **I**ndia | **P**apa | **W**hisky |
| **C**harlie | **J**uliet | **Q**uebec | **X**-ray |
| **D**elta | **K**ilo | **R**omeo | **Y**ankee |
| **E**cho | **L**ima | **S**ierra | **Z**ulu |
| **F**oxtrot | **M**ike | **T**ango | |
| **G**olf | **N**ovember | **U**niform | |

## Weights and measures

| | |
|---|---|
| **Linear measures:** | 1 foot = 30,48 cm; 3 feet = 1 yard;<br>1 mile = 1,760 yards = 1,609 km |
| **Measures of capacity:** | 1 pint = 0.473 litres (US)/0.567 litres (UK); 1 gallon = 3.785 litres (US)/4.540 litres (UK) |
| **Temperature conversion:** | Fahrenheit (F) – Centigrade (Celsius, C)<br>subtract 32 and multiply by 5/9<br>Examples: 32°F ~ 0°C<br>212°F ~ 100°C<br>70°F ~ 21.1°C |



505256

# Answer key

**Unit 1: The travel business**
**1.1 The work of a travel agent**
*1* 1. Applicant should be communicative, speak several languages, be experienced in selling and buying tourist services (mainly Commonwealth), be able to work with different computer programmes. / 2. Friendliness, openness, nice appearance, ...
*2* The work of a travel agent: be prepared to travel world wide, ... / Languages: communicate with tourists, ... / Using the computer: ticketing, ... / Negotiating and contracting skills: with tour operators, ... / Knowledge of geographic and touristic facts: Australia, ...

**1.2 Travel agents and their business partners**
*1* see vocabulary list
*2* 1. Tourist – travel agent – tour operator – producer / tourist – tour operator. / 2. travel agent, producer (airline).
3. Transport: coach, train, ship/ferry. / Accommodation: hotel, motel, .... / Man-made attractions: theme parks, ...

**1.3 At the travel agency**
*1* e.g.: At last I am in Rome. (fact) / Usually they want package holidays.... (habit) / At the moment I am working on a special project. (action happening at the moment)
*2* 1. e.g.: Producers sell tourist services. / 2. generally, often, sometimes, ... / 3. e.g.: Peter is reading a book.

**Office equipment**
*3* a)-8, b)-12, c)-1, d)-5, e)-14, f)-2, g)-10, h)-13, i)-4, j)-11, k)-3, l)-15, m)-9, n)-16, o)-7, p)-6.
*4* All possible, depending on size of travel agency, importance of customer, ...

**Unit 2: Tourism and the tourist industry**
**2.1 The history and development of tourism**
*1* It is Ötzi. He was on his way through the 'Ötztal'. He was a shepherd. Therefore he led his herd up into the mountains, where a sudden change of weather struck him down and he froze to death.
*2* ancient times: Egyptians: first people who travel for pleasure; Greece: Olympic Games = first international tourist event; Romans: thermal and seaside spas, 90,000 kms of roads.
Middle Ages: Marco Polo travels through Asia; pilgrimages to holy sites, (coaching) inns and stagecoach services
18th century: Grand Tour, nature was romanticized.
19th century: attraction of spas in England and Germany; Industrial Revolution: steamboats and trains as new means of transport; Th. Cook: first package holiday
20th century: 1950s: mainly rail travel, 1960s: mainly private car, 1970s: mainly plane, destinations change; today: adventure holidays.
*3* ON HOLIDAY
*4* 1. see examples in grammar box
2. went / had never been / was / had not travelled / took / became / learnt / ate / have not eaten / have always wanted.
3. –

**Future development**
*5* pros: adventure, new experience, ...
cons: too expensive, space sickness, ...
*6* 1. will; 2. will, 3. am going to, 4. will, 5. are you going to do, 6. will.
*7* –

**2.2 Reasons for travelling**
*1* 1) business trip, 2) relaxation, 3) religious reasons, 4) health, 5) sports, 6) meeting people, 7) education.
*2* –
*3* – (for questionnaire see examples)
*4* 'perfect' organization, people know costs in advance, on-site representaive looking after tourists, cheaper (in general), law of country of origin in case of problems, ...

**2.3 Means of transport**
*1* mode of transport: air, water, road, rail.
means of transport: plane, ship/ferry, car/coach, train.
carrier: airline, shipping company, car hire firm/coach company, rail company.
*2* speed: fast, rapid, slow,...
comfort: comfortable, cosy, smooth,...
eco-friendliness: eco-friendly, ...
price: cheap, expensive, reasonable, ...
*3* see model

**2.4 The implications of tourism**
*1* 1) ecological implication, 2) economic implication, 3) sociocultural implication
*2* –
*3* governments of countries of destination: limitation of construction of hotels and touristic infrastructure, strict regulations for behaviour in the country, information for more awareness of local customs.
tour operator/travel agent: information for more awareness of local customs, joint ventures with local tour operators or incoming agencies
tourist: adapt to local customs, behave like a guest, obtain information before trip, respect foreign culture, learn language.

**Unit 3: Giving tourist information about countries and holiday resorts**
**3.1 Tourist information about Kenya**
*1* –
*2* (1) East Africa, (2) north, (3) savannah, fertile lowlands, highlands, (4) Indian Ocean, (5) warmer clothing, (6) cooler mornings, (7) rainwear, (8) Nairobi, (9) Mombasa, (10) Kiswahili, (11) English.
*3* true: 3, 7/ false: 1, 2, 4, 5, 6, 8.
*4* 1. obligation: (e.g.) Health insurance is essential. / advice: (e.g.) Precautions with drinking water are thoroughly recommended. / permission: (e.g.) Cars may be hired from a number of travel agents in Nairobi. / prohibition: (e.g.) Local currency must not be taken out of country.
2. obligation: must, have to, need to, necessary, obligatory, compulsory / advice: to recommend, to advise, to suggest / permission: need not, do not need to, may, do not have to, to allow / prohibition: must not.
3. –
*5* accommodation, facilities, entertainment, local tours, etc.

**3.2 Tourist information about the Hakuna Matata Beach Resort**
*1* 1. round-trip transfer: the transport from the airport to the holiday resort and from the holiday resort back to the airport / on-site representative: an employee of a tour operator, who looks after tourists at their holiday resort.
2. a) water sports, b) water gymnastics.
3. a) alcoholic beverages, b) drugstore, c) pharmacy.
*2* sports: windsurfing, tennis, golfing, water skiing, etc. / facilities: doctor, tourist information office, car rental, supermarket, money exchange office, etc.
*3* –

**Going on safari**
*4* –
*5* a) zebra (6), b) giraffe (3), c) lion (2), d) elephant (7), e) antelope (4), f) crocodile (1), g) hippopotamus (5).
*6* –
*7* 1. a) type I, b) type II, c) type III.
2. 1-d), 2-e), 3-a), 4-b), 5-c)

**Presenting further countries**
*8* –

**Unit 4: Air travel**
**4.1 Some facts about air travel**
*1* true: 2, 3 / false: 1, 4, 5.
*2* 1.– / 2. e.g.: Economy class = the cheapest class of service on a flight.
*3* 1-b), 2-d), 3-e), 4-a), 5-c).

**4.2 Giving information about schedules**
*1* e.g.: Where would you like to travel? – I'd like to visit some friends in Paris. How long would you like to stay? – Three weeks, etc.
*2* 1. 21 mls south of Edmonton.
2. By bus.
3. 45 minutes prior to departure/90 min if baggage is checked through.
4. PAR.
5. Charles de Gaulle.
6. Air Canada.
7. AC 126 + AC 880.
8. Airbus 320 and Boing 747.
9. first class, business class, economy class.
10. No, the flight arrives one day later/the next day.
11. Yes.
12. 1 intermediate stop (on flight AC 880)
*3* –

**Talking about time**
*4* –
*5* see model

**4.3 Ticketing**
*1* 1. International Air Transport Association.
2. scheduled flights = regular flights which are organized by the company that owns the aircraft; charter flights = occasional flights which are usually offered in combination with package tours arranged by the tour operator.
*2* 1. Travellers get their baggage when presenting the ticket (+ sticker).
2. 1) briefcase, 2) handbag/purse, 3) suitcase, 4) trunk, 5) rucksack/backpack, 6) seabag.
*3* evidence of contract of carriage / receipt for accounts department, travel agent, passenger / document for check-in / baggage check.
*4* 1-f), 2-c), 3-m), 4-i), 5-b), 6-l), 7-o), 8-e), 9-n), 10-a), 11-k), 12-p), 13-g), 14-h), 15-d), 16-j).
*5* –

**4.4 At the airport**
*1* e.g.: When does flight no. AC 1371 depart? – Flight no. AC 1371 leaves at 17:45.
*2* 1. departure, 2. landing, 3. international flight, 4. to catch a plane, 5. to be on time, 6. destination.

**Giving directions**
*3* She arrives at the arrivals level (downstairs) and goes straight to the nearest information counter. She goes upstairs and then turns left. Then she walks along this hall past the duty free shop on her left as far as the connecting flights counter. After asking where her connecting flight leaves from, she goes back to the duty free shopping area. After that she goes down this way and takes the first turning on the left, walks on past the children's play area where she has a coffee. After having a coffee, Teresa looks for a money exchange office. She has to go back up to the Air Canada Special Services counter and then goes straight to the office. Unfortunately it is closed. The next one is on the other end of the hall. Therefore she turns around and goes straight to the International Departures Area, where she ends up in front of the money exchange office. Finally she returns to the check-in counter where she meets her friend Paul.

**At the check-in counter**
*4* 1-b), 2-c), 3-c).
*5* (1) luggage, (2) scales, (3) overweight, (4) excess baggage charge, (5) VIP, (6) smoking section, (7) window seat, (8) aisle seat, (9) boarding pass, (10) gate, (11) lounge.

**Unit 5: At the hotel**
**5.1 Staying in New York City**
*1* Yes, because information is completely wrong!
New York City's nick name is The Big Apple. Arriving by boat you will pass The Statue of Liberty and see the skyline dominated by the tower of the Empire State Building.

Having arrived, a modern public transport system of buses and subways takes you everywhere you like, but it is more convenient to stop one of the yellow cabs which are typical for this city.
New York City has a lot of museums as well, one of the most famous is the Guggenheim with its unique architecture which is located on 5th Avenue. Just across the street is Central Park where you can do some roller skating, cycling or simply relax.
5th Avenue is also famous for a lot of boutiques. If you are lucky, you can find a new outfit in which you will be properly dressed for a theatre premiere on Broadway.
New York City offers a large variety of food: Italian food, for example, is best served in Little Italy whereas you can get the best Chinese food in Chinatown.
*2* –

**5.2 Choosing the right accommodation**
*1* 1. tent, caravan/trailer, camper, hut, te(e)pee, igloo, cave, hostel, motel, hotel, etc.
2. **YMCA**: $25 per person/day; **Big Apple Hostel**: double $45 per room/day (dorm-style beds $17 per day); **Mansfield Hotel** (per room/day): single $65, doubles $75, triples $85, quads $118, larges suites $120 for five people, $140 for six.; **The Waldorf-Astoria**: double deluxe: $295–459 plus $40 per person/night (max. 4 adults), suites between $305–865 per suite/night.
*2* Facilities of a first-class hotel: location, … / Rooms: TV, … / Entertainment: floor shows, … / Sports & health: sauna, … / Restaurants/bars: contemporary American Bistro cuisine, … / Services: room service ….
*3* see appendix for substitution table and model letter

**5.3 Food and lodging**
*1* 1. bed & breakfast: breakfast; half board: breakfast, dinner; full board: breakfast, lunch, dinner.
2. Lunch: a meal that you have in the middle of the day. Dinner: the main meal of the day. / Dish: food that is prepared in a particular way and served as a meal. Meal: an occasion such as breakfast, lunch, or dinner, when people eat. / Continental breakfast: a light breakfast that usually consists of bread, butter, jam, and a hot drink, without any cooked food. English breakfast: a breakfast which consists of cooked food, such as bacon & eggs, in addition to toast & marmalade and tea or coffee. / Jam: a food that is made by cooking fruit with a large amount of sugar. Marmalade: a jam-like food made from oranges, or other citrus fruits.
3. British: sausages, toast & marmalade, bacon & eggs, baked beans, orange juice, cereals, scrambled eggs, a cup of tea. / American: French toast, muffins, peanut butter, fried mushrooms, a mug of coffee, orange juice, cereals, fried eggs sunny side up, pancakes & maple syrup.

**A candlelight dinner at the Waldorf-Astoria Bull & Bear**
*2* Being seated / Getting the menu / Ordering / Ordering desserts / Paying / Tipping.
*3* countable: evening, madam, sir, name, table, way, aperitif, candlelight menu, husband, lamb, salmon, main course, soup of the day, shrimp cocktail, side dish, polenta, bottle, meal, dessert, orange cream, cup, bill, room number / uncountable: white wine, Chablis, sparkling water, coffee, tip / but: a bottle of Chablis, a cup of coffee.
*4* I would like to have some sparkling water. (positive sentence) / Would you like some coffee? (questions, when things are offered) / Can you recommend anything? (most questions) / I don't like any dessert. (negative sentence)
*5* –

**5.4 At the reception: telephoning**
*1* **Opening the phonecall:** Reservations. Can I help you?; Can I be of any assistance?; Hello, this is … / **Connecting somebody**: May I talk/speak to …, please?; One moment, please. I'll put you through.; I'll just check that (for you).; Could I have your name, please?; Could you spell that, please?; Could you repeat that, please? / **Saying that someone is not available:** I'm afraid he isn't in at the moment.; I'm sorry, but there is no answer from room no. 301.; Can I take a message?; If you give me your number/name, I'll ask him to call you back.; Would you like to speak to … (instead)?; I'll try again later. / **The line is engaged:** I'm sorry, the line is engaged.; I'm afraid the line is busy at the moment.; OK. I'll hold the line.; I'll try again later. / **Ending the phonecall:** Thanks for calling. Good bye.; Thanks for your help.; Good bye.
*2* –
*3* receiver: the part of a telephone that you hold near your ear and speak into / to dial: press buttons or move the disc on the front of a telephone / yellowpages: a telephone directory in which companies and people are listed under the headings of the kind of business or service that they provide / to hang up: put back the receiver / directory: a book which gives people's names, addresses, and telephone numbers usually arranged in alphabetical order / area code: first part of a telephone number which indicates the region the person lives in / to be cut off: the line is disconnected / operator: a person who works at a telephone exchange or at the switchboard of an office or hotel.

**Unit 6: Rail travel**
**6.1 At the station**
*1* a) restaurant, b) buffet, c) lost and found counter/office, d) luggage/baggage trolley, e) information counter/office, f) ticket office, g) booking office, h) exchange office, i) passenger's/traveler's aid, j) left-luggage office/baggage check room, k) left-luggage lockers, l) post office, m) ladies' toilet, n) gents' toilet, o) waiting room, p) timetable/schedule, q) platform, r) rails/track, s) porter/baggage handler.
*2* a) The porter's trolley is green. / b) The office hours of the information counter are from 9 a.m. to 4 p.m. / c) The dog's leash is too short. / d) The children's luggage has been left at home. / e) The Martins' tickets are invalid. / f) The clock of the station is 5 minutes fast.

**6.2 Touring Britain by train**
*1* 1. station: a building by a railway line where a train stops to pick up passengers and goods/terminus: a large railway station where several routes begin and end
2. Once there were various railway companies in Britain; each company also had a terminus in London.
3. advantages: more competition and therefore lower prices for customers, … / disadvantages: inefficient lines may be closed and as a result railway network is not as dense as before, …
*2* validity & prices: e.g. 8 days = $215 / countries to be visited: England, Scotland and Wales / transfer service: from Heathrow Airport to Paddington Station and from Gatwck Airport to Victoria Station (included in BritRail Pass) / age limit: under 26 (first date of travel) / where to get the pass: BritRail Passes cannot be purchased in Britain / class of carriage: 2nd class only
*3* 1. Tower Bridge, The Millennium Dome
2. e.g. Big Ben, The Tower of London, Houses of Parliament, St. Paul's Cathedral
*4* –
*5* 1. engine, coach, compartment, open-plan seating, luggage rack, washroom, toilet, conference compartment, mother and child compartment, restaurant/ dining car, sleeping car/sleeper, couchette accommodation, berth, luggage van/baggage car
2. compartment seating: families or groups of up to six people can travel among themselves, quieter than open-plan seating, … / open-plan seating: more spacious than compartment, table available for each seat, …
3. modem hook-up, fax machine, cordless phone, photocopier, typewriter, computer socket
4. baby changing facilities, diapers, baby food warmer, baby sitter service, children's playing area
5. couchette accommodation, because it is much cheaper
6. luggage rack: handbag, briefcase, rucksack, sports bag, hatbox, … / baggage car: trunk, surfboard, bike, wardrobe trunk, …
*6* –

**6.3 Special trains**
*1* 1. leaflet or ad, because language is positive and text favours Eurostar
2. civilised, convenient, relaxing, uninterrupted (journey), enjoyable, generous, refreshed / travelling is easy, causes no problems, is quick, …
3. Travelling Eurostar is like gliding through the air and past the country side. There is hardly any noise except a light hiss caused by the speed of the train.
*2* plane: advantage: quick, … / disadvantage: ecologically harmful, …; car or coach & ferry: advantage: own car at hand all the time, inexpensive, … / disadvantage: takes a long time, …; car & motorail (Channel Tunnel): advantage: no delays because of bad weather, … / disadvantage: more expensive than ferry / Note: Eurostar: passenger service only / Le Shuttle: motorail
*3* Georges Nagelmackers created the Orient-Express which started its maiden voyage on 4 October 1883. / The Simplon Tunnel was built in 1906 and in 1921 the Orient-Express ran as far as Istanbul. / 1920s, 1930s: heyday of the legendary train. / From WW II on train service declined and was finally closed down in 1977. / 1982: reopening of the VSOE.
*4* –

**Unit 7: Road travel**
**7.1 Test the West**
*1* 1. 1-j), 2-i), 3-k), 4-g), 5-l), 6-b), 7-f), 8-d), 9-h), 10-a), 11-e), 12-c)
2. true: 3 / false: 1, 2, 4.
3. Disneyland: California, near LA; Yellowstone NP: Wyoming, Rocky Mountains; San Diego: California, border to Mexico; Grand Canyon: Arizona, near Flagstaff; Las Vegas: Nevada; Death Valley NP: California; Hollywood: California, near LA; San Francisco: California; Area 51: Nevada, Groom Lake; Yosemite NP: California; Salt Lake City: Utah; Reno: Nevada, Silicon Valley: California, Palo Alto; Mount Rushmore National Monument (showing 60-ft-tall faces of George Washington, Thomas Jefferson, Abraham Lincoln, Theodore Roosevelt), also called 'shrine of democracy': South Dakota, near Rapid City.
*2* –

**7.2 Renting a car**
*1* 1. A registration number which you must use every time you rent in order to earn points.
2. 1) hatchback; 2) saloon car; 3) estate car.
*2* 1. PAE; 2. LDW; 3. SLI.
*3* Dear …; We would like …; We also provide …; The total amount …; On arrival …; Yours sincerely ….

**7.3 Travelling by coach**
*1* 1. In 2000 it was 86 years old.
2. Because of its sleek design and grey paint.
3. Greyhound serves over 2,400 destinations. Service covers almost the whole nation and Mexico and Canada.
4. Young people can't afford a car; bus travel is cheap. Old people can't / do not want to drive anymore and don't have cars.
*2* a)-8; b)-6; c)-3; d)-9; e)-1; f)-7; g)-4; h)-2; i)-5.
*3* a) The Americruiser has special seats, designed to give firm support and still be comfortable. They are fully adjustable so you can change positions as often as you like. Passengers have more space than on most other motor coaches.
b) You will never have a bumpy trip in a Greyhound Americruiser. You will travel smoothly and comfortably instead, because of a newly developed air-suspension system.
c) Inside, there are overhead parcel racks, so your carry-on luggage is easily accessible.
d) An experienced driver treats you courteously during the trip.
e) Individually controlled reading lights are easy on your eyes.

f) Roomy baggage compartments guarantee that your group will not have to leave anything behind.
g) A convenient on-board restroom is provided.
h) Extra-large tinted picture windows, double glazed and hermetically sealed, allow a great view of the landscape.
i) The Americruiser runs fuel-efficiently due to a quiet diesel engine. So you will be saving our natural resources while enjoying more miles for your money.
4 1-c); 2-e); 3-f); 4-a); 5-b); 6-d); 7-g).
5 rental car: pros: flexible, independent, … / cons: expensive, driver can't relax or enjoy landscape, …
coach: pros: cheap, 24-hour service, sleeping on coach possible, … / cons: dependent on routes and timetable, no privacy, ….
6 see appendix for substitution table and model letter

**Touring the USA by Greyhound**
7 –
8 –

**Unit 8: Ship Cruises**
**8.1 Cruising the Hawaiian Islands**
1 1. SAT: embarkation, unpacking luggage, enjoying evening on board / SUN: exploring ship, show at night / MON: excursion to Kauai / TUE+WED: relaxing on deck, excursion to Maui / THU+FRI: excursions to Hawaii / SAT: excursion to Honolulu.
2. –
2 1. –
2. a) the USA / 50th State; b) Hawaii, Honolulu (Oahu); c) a wreath of flowers, leaves, etc. worn around the neck; d) Pearl Harbor: Dec. 7, 1941: The Japanese open hostilities with a surprise attack: Waves of Japanese dive-bombers and torpedo planes thundered across the Hawaiian island of Oahu, bombing ships at anchor in Pearl Harbor and strafing planes parked at nearby air bases. American forces suffered their most devastating loss in history. In less than three hours eight battleships, three light cruisers and two destroyers had been sunk or crippled, and 360 aircraft destroyed or damaged. More than 2,000 Americans died.
USS Arizona National Monument: an austere, three-part structure built over the sunken battleship in which over a thousand servicemen perished.

**8.2 On board the MS Patriot**
1 1. capacity: 1,214 passengers; weight: 33,930 gross tons; length: 704 ft = 214,6 m.
2. a) see Unit 5.2; b) Cabins: queen-sized bed, … / Entertainment: stage, … / Restaurants & bars: captain's dinner, … / Sports & Health: wading pool, … / Services: destination service, …
3. a) Because it is the middle deck. b) whirlpool: People sit in it, etc. / wading pool: People wade/walk in it. c) No! gift shop: presents, gifts; drugstore: medicine, shower gel, etc. d) stage at bow: theatre plays, concerts, movies; stage at mid ship: bands e) bow and stern f) two elevators near the photo gallery, four mid ship, one near projection room.
2 1. true: 3 / false: 1, 2, 4.
2. a) water and horizon b) No, it is a large window that allows a panoramic view. c) bathtub, because you can stretch your legs.
3 –

**8.3 Dealing with complaints**
1 1. Day 2: Bad sea food made them vomit. / Day 4: Mr Duckworth broke his leg due to slippery deck. / Day 6: Cabin flooded due to leaking porthole window. Clothes got soaked, therefore no dress for captain's dinner.
2. Day 2: Chef, because he is responsible for food. / Day 4: Purser, because he looks after passengers' general comfort. / Day 6: Captain, because the Duckworths are fed up.
3. –
2 see appendix

**Cruising the world**
3 –
4 –

## Vocabulary per unit

**Unit 1: The travel business**
**1.1 The work of a travel agent**
ad(vertisement) – Annonce
applicant – Bewerber
application – Bewerbung
benefit package – Sozialleistungen
contract, to – kontraktieren
negotiate, to – verhandeln
salary – Gehalt
skill – Fertigkeit
travel agent – Reisemittler
travel benefit – Reisevergünstigung

**1.2 Travel agents and their business partners**
accommodation – Unterkunft
at the request of – auf Anfrage von
chain of distribution – Vertriebskette
coach – Reisebus
commission – Gebühr
demand – Nachfrage
in bulk – im Großen
link – hier: (Ketten-)Glied
man-made attraction – künstliche Attraktion
package holiday – Pauschalreise
producer – Leistungsträger
tour operator – Reiseveranstalter

**1.3 At the travel agency**
apprentice – Auszubildender
assistant – Mitarbeiter
available – verfügbar
brochure – Broschüre
calculator – Taschenrechner
catalogue – Katalog
filing cabinet – Aktenschrank
habit – Gewohnheit
keyboard – Tastatur
local – vor Ort / örtlich
map – Landkarte
native – Einheimischer
offer – Angebot
office hours – Bürozeiten
printer – Drucker
rental car – Mietwagen
scooter – Motorroller
tour guide – Reiseführer
trainee – Praktikant
wastepaper bin – Papierkorb

**Unit 2: Tourism and the tourist industry**
**2.1 The history and development of tourism**
access tube – Zugangsröhre
affordable – erschwinglich
ancient – altertümlich
approximately – ungefähr
bold – dreist, mutig
consciousness – Bewusstsein
decade – Jahrzehnt
destination – Ziel
development – Entwicklung
dock, to – anlegen
doubt – Zweifel
expect, to – erwarten
explorer – Entdecker
frontier – Grenze
holy site – heilige Stätte
inn – Herberge
invent, to – erfinden
key event – Schlüsselereignis
launch, to – schleudern
likely – wahrscheinlich
long-haul journey – Fernreise
medieval – mittelalterlich
merchant – Händler
orbit, to – umkreisen
pilgrim – Pilger
pleasure – Vergnügen
purpose – Zweck
record, to – aufzeichnen
scone – engl. Gebäck
spa – (Heil-)Bad
spring – Quelle
stagecoach – Postkutsche
steam engine – Dampfmaschine
vehicle – Gefährt
weightlessness – Schwerelosigkeit

**2.2 Reasons for travelling**
choice – Auswahl
occupation – Beruf
questionnaire – Fragebogen

**2.3 Means of transport**
carrier – Transportunternehmen
eco-friendliness – Umweltfreundlichkeit
mode of transport – Transportart

**2.4 The implications of tourism**
concerned, to be – betroffen sein
convince, to – überzeugen
country of destination – Zielland
impact – Einfluss
implication – Auswirkung
responsible, to be – verantwortlich sein

**Unit 3: Giving tourist information about countries and holiday resorts**
**3.1 Tourist information about Kenya**
advice – Ratschlag
advisable – ratsam
altitude – Höhe
application – hier: Antrag
arid – dürr
avoid, to – vermeiden
compulsory – obligatorisch
convenient – bequem
currency – Währung
denomination – Nennbetrag
embassy – Botschaft
endemic – endemisch
endorse, to – billigen
enquire, to – anfragen
entry permit – Einreisegenehmigung
entry regulations – Einreisebestimmungen
exception – Ausnahme
extension – Verlängerung
fertile – fruchtbar
holiday resort – Ferienort/-anlage
infect, to – infizieren
insure, to – versichern
issue, to – ausstellen
means of payment – Zahlungsmittel
merchant – Handels-
obligation – Verpflichtung
onward connection – Weiterverbindung
operate, to – betreiben
permission – Erlaubnis
precaution – Vorsichtsmaßnahme
prohibit, to – verbieten
prohibition – Verbot
provide, to – zur Verfügung stellen
recommend, to – empfehlen
renewal – Erneuerung
require, to – benötigen
scheduled flight – Linienflug
shore – Ufer

| | |
|---|---|
| stagnant | – stehend |
| suggest, to | – vorschlagen |
| suspend, to | – einstellen |
| temper, to | – temperieren |
| temperate | – gemäßigt |
| travel requirements | – Reiseanforderungen |
| vaccination certificate | – Impfbescheinigung |
| valid | – gültig |

**3.2 Tourist information about the Hakuna Matata Beach Resort**

| | |
|---|---|
| achieve, to | – erreichen |
| beverage | – Getränk |
| deep-sea fishing | – Hochseefischen |
| drugstore | – Drogerie |
| enchant, to | – entzücken |
| exceed, to | – übertreffen |
| facility | – Einrichtung |
| fresh-water | – Süßwasser |
| habitat | – Lebensraum |
| hesitate, to | – zögern |
| itinerary | – Reiseplan |
| on-site representative | – Zielgebietsvertreter |
| overnight stay | – Übernachtung |
| pharmacy | – Apotheke |
| plaster | – Pflaster |
| present, to | – präsentieren |
| presentation | – Vortrag |
| reserve | – Reservat |
| scuba diving | – Tauchen |
| snorkeling | – Schnorcheln |
| stalk | – Pirsch |

**Unit 4: Air travel**

**4.1 Some facts about air travel**

| | |
|---|---|
| advance reservation | – Vorabreservierung |
| approve, to | – anerkennen |
| booked up, to be | – ausgebucht sein |
| collect, to | – hier: abholen |
| confirm, to | – bestätigen |
| connecting flight | – Anschlussflug |
| deposit | – Anzahlung |
| direct flight | – Direktflug |
| economy class | – Touristenklasse |
| minimum connecting time | – Mindestumsteigezeit |
| return flight | – (Hin- und) Rückflug |
| round trip | – Hin- und Rückflug |
| single flight | – Hinflug |
| take-off | – Start |
| take off, to | – starten |

**4.2 Giving information about schedules**

| | |
|---|---|
| abbreviation | – Abkürzung |
| arrival | – Ankunft |
| check-in | – Abfertigung |
| class of service | – Buchungsklasse |
| departure | – hier: Abflug |
| destination | – Bestimmungsort |
| en route | – unterwegs |
| eta: estimated time of arrival | – voraussichtliche Ankunftszeit |
| etd: estimated time of departure | – voraussichtliche Abflugzeit |
| GMT | – Greenwich Mean Time |
| intermediate stop | – Zwischenlandung |
| local time | – Ortszeit |
| origin | – hier: Abflugort |
| schedule | – (Flug-)Plan |
| timetable | – (Flug-)Plan |

**4.3 Ticketing**

| | |
|---|---|
| accounts department | – Buchhaltungsabteilung |
| amendment charge | – Umbuchungsgebühr |
| audit-coupon | – Buchhaltungsbeleg |
| baggage check | – Gepäckschein |
| cancellation charge | – Stornogebühr |
| conditions of carriage | – Beförderungsbedingungen |
| contract | – Vertrag |
| coupon | – Schein/Beleg |
| fee | – Gebühr |
| free baggage allowance | – zulässiges Freigepäck |
| indicate, to | – (an-)zeigen |
| occasional | – gelegentlich |
| purchase, to | – kaufen |
| rebook, to | – umbuchen |
| regular | – regelmäßig |
| scheduled air service | – Linienflug |
| tax | – Steuer |
| ticketing | – Tickets ausstellen |
| voluntary | – freiwillig |

**4.4 At the airport**

| | |
|---|---|
| airline | – Fluggesellschaft |
| aisle seat | – Sitz am Gang |
| baggage claim | – Gepäckabholung |
| board, to | – an Bord gehen |
| boarding pass | – Bordkarte |
| customs | – Zoll |
| delayed, to be | – verspätet sein |
| domestic flight | – Inlandsflug |
| excess baggage | – Übergepäck |
| fare | – Fahrpreis |
| lounge | – Warteraum |
| luggage | – Gepäck |
| on duty, to be | – im Dienst sein |
| on time | – pünktlich |
| overweight | – übergewichtig (Gepäck) |
| proceed, to | – hier: weitergehen |
| scale(s) | – Waage |
| section | – Bereich |
| turning | – Abzweig |

**Unit 5: At the hotel**

**5.1 Staying in New York City**

| | |
|---|---|
| convenient | – zweckmäßig |
| cross-check, to | – gegenprüfen |
| honeymoon | – Hochzeitsreise |
| nickname | – Kosename |
| subway | – hier: U-Bahn |
| unique | – einzigartig |
| variety | – Auswahl |
| Victory Column | – Siegessäule |

**5.2 Choosing the right accommodation**

| | |
|---|---|
| appointed, to be | – ausgestattet sein |
| benefit | – Vorteil |
| budget-style | – preisgünstig |
| celebrated | – berühmt |
| chop | – Kotelett |
| concierge | – Portier |
| contemporary | – zeitgenössisch |
| convivial | – gesellig |
| deepen, to | – vertiefen |
| dignified | – ehrwürdig |
| discriminating | – verwöhnt |
| distinctive | – unverkennbar |
| distinguished | – vornehm, gepflegt |
| dorm-style bed | – Etagenbett |
| double (room) | – Doppelzimmer |
| eminent | – ausgesprochen |
| establishment | – Einrichtung |
| executive | – hier: gehoben |
| exquisite | – ausgezeichnet |
| gambling | – Glücksspiel |
| grace | – Anmut |
| hallway | – Flur |
| hefty | – saftig |
| impeccable | – tadellos |
| indulge, to | – verwöhnen |
| jacuzzi | – Whirlpool |
| king (size) | – extra groß |
| landmark | – Wahrzeichen |
| lobby | – Empfangshalle |
| locker | – Schließfach |
| modem hook-up | – Modemanschluss |
| myriad | – große Menge |
| oak | – Eiche |
| occupancy | – Belegung |
| occupy, to | – belegen |
| quad | – 4-Bett-Zimmer |
| quote, to | – angeben |
| replete with | – reichlich ausgestattet mit |
| single (room) | – Einzelzimmer |
| state-of-the-art | – hochmodern |
| subject to, to be | – unterworfen sein |
| triple (room) | – 3-Bett-Zimmer |
| turn-of-the-century | – Jahrhundertwende |
| YMCA: Young Men's Christian Association | – Christlicher Verein Junger Menschen |

**5.3 Food and lodging**

| | |
|---|---|
| bill | – Rechnung |
| catering | – Verpflegung |
| celery root | – Selleriewurzel |
| cereals | – Cerealien |
| dinner | – Hauptmahlzeit |
| dish | – Gericht, Geschirr |
| fennel | – Fenchel |
| French toast | – armer Ritter |
| fried eggs sunny side up | – Spiegeleier |
| full board | – Vollpension |
| half board | – Halbpension |
| lodging | – Unterkunft |
| lunch | – Mittagessen |
| main course | – Hauptgang |
| maple syrup | – Ahornsirup |
| mug | – (Kaffee-)Pott |
| mushroom | – Pilz |
| rosemary | – Rosmarin |
| salmon | – Lachs |
| scrambled eggs | – Rührei |
| side dish | – Beilage |
| sparkling water | – Mineralwasser |
| starter | – Vorspeise |
| tarragon | – Estragon |
| tip | – Trinkgeld |

**5.4 At the reception: telephoning**

| | |
|---|---|
| ant | – Ameise |
| area code | – Vorwahl |
| busy, to be | – hier: besetzt sein |
| callout | – Ausruf; hier: Sprechblase |
| chambermaid | – Zimmermädchen |
| directory | – Telefonbuch |
| engaged, to be | – hier: besetzt sein |
| operator | – Vermittlung |
| put somebody through, to | – jmd. verbinden mit |
| receiver | – Hörer |
| yellow pages | – Branchenbuch |

**Unit 6: Rail travel**

**6.1 At the station**

| | |
|---|---|
| baggage check room (AE) | – Gepäckaufbewahrung |
| baggage handler (AE) | – Gepäckträger |
| baggage trolley (AE) | – Gepäckwagen/Kofferkuli |
| blocked, to be | – verstopft sein |
| buffet | – Imbiss |
| cockroach | – Kakerlake |
| leash | – (Hunde-)Leine |
| left-luggage locker | – Schließfach |
| left-luggage office | – Gepäckaufbewahrung |
| lost and found counter/office | – Fundbüro |
| luggage trolley (BE) | – Gepäckwagen / Kofferkuli |
| passenger's aid (BE) | – Bahnhofsmission |
| platform | – Bahnsteig |
| porter (BE) | – Gepäckträger |
| rails (BE) | – Gleis/Schienen |
| track (AE) | – Gleis/Schienen |
| traveler's aid (AE) | – Bahnhofsmission |

**6.2 Touring Britain by train**

| | |
|---|---|
| access | – Zugang |
| age limit | – Altersbeschränkung |
| baggage car | – Gepäckwagen |
| berth | – Koje |
| bulky | – sperrig |
| car/coach | – Wagen/Waggon |
| class of carriage | – Beförderungsklasse |
| compartment | – Abteil |
| conference compartment | – Konferenzabteil |



505260

| | |
|---|---|
| consecutive | – aufeinander folgend |
| constitute, to | – hier: darstellen |
| couchette car | – Liegewagen |
| dining car | – Speisewagen |
| duration | – Dauer |
| engine | – hier: Lokomotive |
| entire | – gesamt |
| globetrotter | – Weltenbummler |
| luggage rack | – Gepäckablage |
| luggage van | – Gepäckwagen |
| mother and child compartment | – Mutter-Kind-Abteil |
| open-plan car | – Großraumwagen |
| purchase, to | – kaufen |
| refreshment | – Erfrischung |
| requirement | – Erfordernis |
| restaurant car | – Speisewagen |
| restful | – erholsam |
| sleeping car | – Schlafwagen |
| splendid | – herrlich |
| terminus/termini (pl) | – Kopfbahnhof/-höfe |
| terrific | – sagenhaft |
| validity | – Gültigkeit |

**6.3 Special trains**

| | |
|---|---|
| beyond | – jenseits |
| bygone era | – längst vergangene Zeiten |
| celebrity | – Berühmtheit |
| civilized | – kultiviert |
| cruise ship | – Kreuzfahrtschiff |
| decline, to | – verfallen |
| extended | – verlängert |
| fortune | – Glück |
| generous | – großzügig |
| gradually | – allmählich |
| heyday | – Blütezeit |
| hike | – Wanderung |
| inaugurate, to | – hier: einweihen |
| in full swing, to be | – in vollem Schwung sein |
| initial | – anfänglich |
| maiden run | – Jungfernfahrt |
| mobile phone | – Mobiltelefon |
| onset | – Beginn |
| queue | – (Warte-)Schlange |
| significant(ly) | – bedeutend |
| sumptuous | – üppig |
| trace back, to | – zurückverfolgen |
| whisper, to | – flüstern; hier (poet.): säuseln |

**Unit 7: Road travel**

**7.1 Test the West**

| | |
|---|---|
| breast implant | – Brustimplantat |
| cable car | – Straßenbahn |
| divorce | – Scheidung |
| giant redwood | – Mammutbaum |
| instant | – sofort |
| spouting geysers | – speiende Geysire |

**7.2 Renting a car**

| | |
|---|---|
| account | – Konto |
| award-winning | – preisgekrönt |
| car rental | – Autovermietung |
| claim | – Anspruch |
| confirm, to | – bestätigen |
| confirmation (letter of ~) | – Bestätigung (-sschreiben) |
| cover, to | – decken |
| decline, to | – hier: ablehnen |
| draw from, to | – einziehen |
| enrollment form | – Anmeldeformular |
| estate car (BE) | – Kombiwagen |
| expire, to | – ablaufen |
| familiar with, to be | – vertraut sein mit |
| hatchback | – 5-Tür-Wagen |
| insurance | – Versicherung |
| issue, to | – ausstellen |
| liability insurance | – Haftpflichtversicherung |
| Loss Damage Waiver (LDW) | – Kaskoversicherung |
| market value | – Marktwert |
| membership number | – Mitgliedsnummer |
| mistress | – hier: Frauchen |
| optional | – freiwillig |
| Personal Accident and Effects Insurance (PAE) | – Insassenversicherung |
| preference | – Vorliebe |
| property | – Besitz |
| protection | – Schutz |
| recover, to | – hier: wiederbeschaffen |
| reimburse, to | – entschädigen |
| relieve, to | – entbinden von |
| rent, to | – mieten |
| rental contract | – Mietvertrag |
| rental terms | – Mietbedingungen |
| revenue | – Einnahmen |
| saloon car (BE) | – Limousine |
| sedan (AE) | – Limousine |
| station wagon (AE) | – Kombiwagen |
| Supplemental Liability Insurance (SLI) | – Zusatzhaftpflichtversicherung |
| third-party insurance | – Haftpflichtversicherung |
| waive, to | – verzichten auf |

**7.3 Travelling by coach**

| | |
|---|---|
| accessible | – zugänglich |
| adjustable | – anpassbar |
| air-suspension | – Luftfederung |
| assign, to | – zuweisen |
| blanket | – Decke |
| bumpy | – holperig |
| carry-on luggage | – Handgepäck |
| cellular phone | – Mobiltelefon |
| contiguous | – aneinander grenzend |
| courteous | – höflich |
| customer advisory talk | – Kundenberatungsgespräch |
| double glazed | – doppelverglast |
| dub, to | – hier: taufen (Spitzname) |
| encompass, to | – umfassen |
| eventful | – ereignisreich |
| federal | – Bundes- |
| firm | – stabil |
| fleet | – Flotte |
| fuel-efficient | – benzinsparend |
| hard | – schwer |
| hardly | – kaum |
| headquarter | – Hauptgeschäftsstelle |
| miner | – Minenarbeiter |
| pillow | – Kissen |
| recline, to | – zurücklehnen |
| restroom | – Toilette |
| rural | – ländlich |
| senior citizen | – älterer (Mit-)Bürger |
| setting | – Schauplatz |
| sleek | – schlank |
| smooth | – glatt, weich |
| stopover | – Zwischenstopp |
| tinted | – getönt |
| tire (AE)/ tyre (BE) | – Reifen |
| trademark | – (Handels-)Marke |
| urban | – städtisch |

**Unit 8: Ship cruises**

**8.1 Cruising the Hawaiian Islands**

| | |
|---|---|
| bask, to | – sich aalen |
| beckon, to | – winken |
| buzz | – hier: Gemurmel |
| curvaceous | – kurvenreich |
| deck chair | – Liegestuhl |
| dip, to | – eintauchen |
| embark, to | – einschiffen |
| farewell | – Abschied |
| fragrant | – duftend |
| glittering | – glitzernd |
| hearty | – herzhaft, kräftig |
| horizon | – Horizont |
| join in, to | – mitmachen |
| lei | – Blumenkette |
| lush | – saftig, üppig |
| nap | – Nickerchen |
| peak | – Gipfel |
| port | – Hafen |
| retire, to | – hier: in den Ruhestand treten |
| round out, to | – abrunden |
| secluded | – abgeschieden |
| snow-capped | – schneebedeckt |
| spark, to | – versprühen |
| stargaze, to | – in die Sterne schauen |
| trolley | – hier: kleiner Bus |
| unspoiled | – unberührt |

**8.2 On board the MS Patriot**

| | |
|---|---|
| bathtub | – Badewanne |
| bow | – Bug |
| elevator (AE), lift (BE) | – Fahrstuhl |
| float, to | – schwimmen, treiben |
| gross ton | – Bruttoregistertonne |
| ground plan | – Grundriss |
| interior | – innen |
| ocean view | – Meerblick |
| outrigger | – Ausleger |
| parlo(u)r | – Salon |
| picture window | – Panoramafenster |
| porthole window | – Bullauge |
| stateroom | – Kabine |
| stern | – Heck |
| superior | – höherwertig |
| wade, to | – waten |

**8.3 Dealing with complaints**

| | |
|---|---|
| apologize, to | – sich entschuldigen |
| apology | – Entschuldigung |
| challenge | – Herausforderung |
| chef | – Koch, Küchenchef |
| complain, to | – sich beschweren |
| complaint | – Beschwerde |
| Greater Antilles | – Große Antillen |
| jellyfish | – Qualle |
| Lesser Antilles | – Kleine Antillen |
| purser | – Zahlmeister/Chefsteward |
| shipping company | – Reederei |

**Appendix**

**The layout of a business letter**

| | |
|---|---|
| attention (line) | – hier: zu Händen |
| carbon copy | – Durchschlag |
| complimentary close | – Schlussformel |
| enclosure | – Anlage |
| post code | – Postleitzahl (GB) |
| recipient | – Empfänger |
| reference | – Bezug |
| salutation (line) | – Anrede(-zeile) |
| subject (line) | – Betreff(-zeile) |
| yours faithfully | – Mit freundl. Grüßen |
| yours sincerely | – Mit freundl. Grüßen |
| yours truly | – Mit freundl. Grüßen |
| ZIP (Zone Improvement Plan) code | – Postleitzahl (USA) |

**Enquiry (BE)/Inquiry (AE)**

| | |
|---|---|
| appreciate, to | – schätzen |
| enquiry (inquiry) | – Anfrage |
| in due course | – zu gegebener Zeit |
| reply | – Antwort |

**Offer**

| | |
|---|---|
| appeal to sb, to | – gefallen |
| at your disposal, to be | – zur Verfügung stehen |
| convenience | – Annehmlichkeit |
| expectation | – Erwartung |
| fitted, to be | – ausgestattet sein |
| furnished, to be | – möbliert sein |
| hesitate, to | – zögern |
| offer | – Angebot |
| request, to | – anfragen |
| submit, to | – unterbreiten |
| suit, to | – hier: entsprechen |
| supply, to | – bereitstellen |

**Confirmation**
confirmation – Bestätigung
due, to be – fällig sein
get in touch, to – kontaktieren

**Cancellation**
cancellation – Storno
circumstances – Umstände
owing to sth – aufgrund
unforeseen – unvorhergesehen

**Complaint**
by return of post – postwendend
compensation – Entschädigung
complaint – Beschwerde
considerable – beträchtlich
receive, to – empfangen
reduction – Minderung
rude – unfreundlich
safety standards – Sicherheitsstandards
satisfaction – Zufriedenheit
settle, to – hier: klären

**Application**
application – Bewerbung
apply, to – bewerben
certificate – Zeugnis
Chamber of Commerce – Industrie- und Handelskammer
command – hier: Beherrschung
corporate travel – Firmenreisedienst
curriculum vitae (CV) – Lebenslauf (GB)
gain, to – erlangen
post – Stelle
résumé – Lebenslauf (USA)
word-processing program(me) – Textverarbeitungsprogramm

**Résumé or CV**
A-levels – Abitur
education – Schulbildung
graduation – (Schul-)Abschluss
intended for, to be – bestimmt sein für
marital status – Familienstand

nanny – Kindermädchen
reference – hier: Empfehlung

**Giving a presentation**
audience – Publikum
encyclopedia – Lexikon
outline – Gliederung
presentation – Vortrag
slide – Dia
source – Quelle
support, to – unterstützen
tourist board – Fremdenverkehrsamt
wall news-sheet – Wandzeitung

**Weights and measures**
conversion – Umrechnung
linear measure – Längenmaß
measure – Maß
measure of capacity – Hohlmaß
weight – Gewicht

## Vocabulary in alphabetical order

**A**
abbreviation – Abkürzung
access – Zugang
accessible – zugänglich
access tube – Zugangsröhre
accommodation – Unterkunft
account – Konto
accounts department – Buchhaltung
achieve, to – erreichen
ad(vertisement) – Annonce
adjustable – anpassbar
advance reservation – Vorabreservierung
advice – Ratschlag
advisable – ratsam
affordable – erschwinglich
age limit – Altersbegrenzung
airline – Fluggesellschaft
air-suspension – Luftfederung
aisle seat – Sitz am Gang
A-levels – Abitur
altitude – Höhe
amendment charge – Umbuchungsgebühr
ancient – altertümlich
ant – Ameise
apologize, to – sich entschuldigen
apology – Entschuldigung
appeal to sb, to – gefallen
applicant – Bewerber
application – Bewerbung
apply, to – bewerben
appointed, to be – ausgestattet sein
appreciate, to – schätzen
apprentice – Auszubildender
approve, to – anerkennen
approximately – ungefähr
area code – Vorwahl
arid – dürr
arrival – Ankunft
assign, to – zuweisen
assistant – Mitarbeiter
at the request of – auf Anfrage von
at your disposal, to be – Ihnen zur Verfügung stehen
attention (line) – hier: zu Händen
audience – Publikum
audit-coupon – Buchhaltungsbeleg
available – verfügbar
avoid, to – vermeiden
award-winning – preisgekrönt

**B**
baggage car (AE) – Gepäckwagen
baggage check – Gepäckschein
baggage check room (AE) – Gepäckaufbewahrung
baggage claim – Gepäckabholung
baggage handler (AE) – Kofferträger
baggage trolley (AE) – Gepäckwagen/Kofferkuli
bask, to – sich aalen
bathtub – Badewanne
beckon, to – winken
benefit – Vorteil
benefit package – Sozialleistungen
berth – Koje
beverage – Getränk
beyond – jenseits
bill – Rechnung
blanket – Decke
blocked, to be – verstopft sein
board, to – an Bord gehen
boarding pass – Bordkarte
bold – dreist, mutig
booked up, to be – ausgebucht sein
bow – Bug
breast implant – Brustimplantat
brochure – Broschüre
budget-style – preisgünstig
buffet – Imbiss
bulky – sperrig
bumpy – holperig
busy, to be – hier: besetzt sein
buzz – hier: Gemurmel
bygone era – längst vergangene Zeiten
by return of post – postwendend

**C**
cable car – Straßenbahn
calculator – Taschenrechner
callout – Ausruf; hier: Sprechblase
cancellation – Storno
cancellation charge – Stornogebühr
car/coach – Waggon
carbon copy – Durchschlag
car rental – Autovermietung
carrier – Transportunternehmen
carry-on luggage – Handgepäck
catalog(ue) – Katalog
catering – Verpflegung
celebrated – berühmt
celebrity – Berühmtheit
celery root – Selleriewurzel
cellular phone – Mobiltelefon
cereals – Cerealien
certificate – Zeugnis
chain of distribution – Vertriebskette
challenge – Herausforderung
Chamber of Commerce – Industrie- und Handelskammer
chambermaid – Zimmermädchen
check-in – Abfertigung
chef – Küchenchef, Koch
choice – Auswahl
chop – Kotelett
circumstances – Umstände
civilized – kultiviert
claim – Anspruch
class of carriage – Beförderungsklasse
class of service – Buchungsklasse
coach – Reisebus
cockroach – Kakerlake
collect, to – hier: abholen
command – hier: Beherrschung
commission – Gebühr
compartment – Abteil
compensation – Entschädigung
complain, to – sich beschweren
complaint – Beschwerde
complimentary close – Schlussformel
compulsory – obligatorisch
concerned, to be – betroffen sein
concierge – Portier
conditions of carriage – Beförderungsbedingungen
conference compartment – Konferenzabteil
confirm, to – bestätigen
confirmation (letter of ~) – Bestätigung(-sschreiben)
connecting flight – Anschlussflug
consciousness – Bewusstsein
consecutive – aufeinander folgend
considerable – beträchtlich
constitute, to – hier: darstellen
contemporary – zeitgenössisch
contiguous – aneinander grenzend
contract – Vertrag
contract, to – kontraktieren
convenience – Annehmlichkeit
convenient – bequem
conversion – Umrechnung
convince, to – überzeugen
convivial – gesellig
corporate travel – Firmenreisedienst
couchette car – Liegewagen
country of destination – Zielland
coupon – Schein/Beleg
courteous – höflich
cover, to – decken
cross-check, to – gegenprüfen
cruise ship – Kreuzfahrtschiff
currency – Währung
curriculum vitae (CV) – Lebenslauf
curvaceous – kurvenreich
customer advisory talk – Kundenberatungsgespräch
customs – Zoll



505262

**D**

decade – Jahrzehnt
deck chair – Liegestuhl
decline, to – verfallen
deepen, to – vertiefen
deep-sea fishing – Hochseeangeln
delayed, to be – verspätet sein
demand – Nachfrage
denomination – Nennbetrag
departure – hier: Abflug
deposit – Anzahlung
destination – Bestimmungsort
development – Entwicklung
dignified – ehrwürdig
dining car – Speisewagen
dinner – Hauptmahlzeit
dip, to – eintauchen
direct flight – Direktflug
directory – Telefonbuch
discriminating – verwöhnt
dish – Gericht, Geschirr
distinctive – unverkennbar
distinguished – vornehm gepflegt
divorce – Scheidung
dock, to – anlegen
domestic flight – Inlandsflug
dorm-style bed – Etagenbett
double (room) – Doppelzimmer
double glazed – doppelverglast
doubt – Zweifel
draw from, to – einziehen
drugstore – Drogerie
dub, to – hier: taufen (Spitzname)
due, to be – fällig sein
duration – Dauer

**E**

eco-friendliness – Umweltfreundlichkeit
economy class – Touristenklasse
education – Schulbildung
elevator (AE) – Fahrstuhl
embark, to – einschiffen
embassy – Botschaft
eminent – ausgesprochen
enchant, to – verzaubern
enclosure – Anlage
encompass, to – umfassen
encyclopedia – Lexikon
endemic – endemisch
endorse, to – billigen
engaged, to be – hier: besetzt sein
engine – hier: Lokomotive
enquire, to – anfragen
enquiry (inquiry) – Anfrage
enrollment form – Anmeldeformular
en route – unterwegs
entire – gesamt
entry permit – Einreisegenehmigung
entry regulations – Einreisebestimmungen
establishment – Einrichtung
estate car (BE) – Kombiwagen
eta: estimated time of arrival – voraussichtliche Ankunftszeit
etd: estimated time of departure – voraussichtliche Abflugzeit
eventful – ereignisreich
exceed, to – übertreffen
exception – Ausnahme
excess baggage – Übergepäck
executive – hier: gehoben
expect, to – erwarten
expectation – Erwartung
expire, to – ablaufen
explorer – Entdecker
exquisite – ausgezeichnet
extended – verlängert
extension – Verlängerung

**F**

facility – Einrichtung
familiar with, to be – vertraut sein mit
fare – Fahrpreis
farewell – Abschied
federal – Bundes-
fee – Gebühr
fennel – Fenchel
fertile – fruchtbar
filing cabinet – Aktenschrank
firm – stabil
fitted, to be – ausgestattet sein
fleet – Flotte
float, to – schwimmen, treiben
fortune – Glück
fragrant – duftend
free baggage allowance – zulässiges Freigepäck
French toast – armer Ritter
fresh-water – Süßwasser
fried eggs sunny side up – Spiegeleier
frontier – Grenze
fuel-efficient – benzinsparend
full board – Vollpension
furnished, to be – möbliert sein

**G**

gain, to – erlangen
gambling – Glücksspiel
generous – großzügig
get in touch, to – kontaktieren
giant redwood – Mammutbaum
glittering – glitzernd
globetrotter – Weltenbummler
GMT – Greenwich Mean Time
grace – Anmut
gradually – allmählich
graduation – (Schul-)Abschluss
Greater Antilles – Große Antillen
gross ton – Bruttoregistertonne
ground plan – Grundriss

**H**

habit – Gewohnheit
habitat – Lebensraum
half board – Halbpension
hallway – Flur
hard – schwer
hardly – kaum
hatchback – 5-Tür-Wagen
headquarter – Hauptgeschäftsstelle
hearty – herzhaft, kräftig
hefty – saftig
hesitate, to – zögern
heyday – Blütezeit
hike – Wanderung
holiday resort – Ferienort/-anlage
holy site – heilige Stätte
honeymoon – Hochzeitsreise
horizon – Horizont

**I**

impact – Einfluss
impeccable – tadellos
implication – Auswirkung
inaugurate, to – hier: einweihen
in bulk – im Großen
indicate, to – (an-)zeigen
in due course – zu gegebener Zeit
indulge, to – verwöhnen
infect, to – infizieren
in full swing, to be – in vollem Schwung sein
initial – anfänglich
inn – Herberge
instant – sofort
insurance – Versicherung
insure, to – versichern
intended for, to be – bestimmt sein für
interior – innen
intermediate stop – Zwischenlandung
invent, to – erfinden
issue, to – ausstellen
itinerary – Reiseplan

**J**

jacuzzi – Whirlpool
jellyfish – Qualle
join (in) to – mitmachen

**K**

keyboard – Tastatur
key event – Schlüsselereignis
king (size) – extra groß

**L**

landmark – Wahrzeichen
launch, to – schleudern
leash – (Hunde-)Leine
left-luggage locker – Schließfach
left-luggage office – Gepäckaufbewahrung
lei – Blumenkette
Lesser Antilles – Kleine Antillen
liability insurance – Haftpflichtversicherung
likely – wahrscheinlich
linear measure – Längenmaß
link – hier: (Ketten-)Glied
lobby – Empfangshalle
local – vor Ort, örtlich
local time – Ortszeit
locker – Schließfach
lodging – Unterkunft
long-haul journey – Fernreise
Loss Damage Waiver (LDW) – Kaskoversicherung
lost and found counter/office – Fundbüro
lounge – Warteraum
luggage (BE) – Gepäck
luggage rack – Gepäckablage
luggage trolley (BE) – Gepäckwagen, Kofferkuli
luggage van (BE) – Gepäckwagen
lunch – Mittagessen
lush – saftig, üppig

**M**

maiden run – Jungfernfahrt
main course – Hauptgang
man-made attraction – künstliche Attraktion
map – Landkarte
maple syrup – Ahornsirup
marital status – Familienstand
market value – Marktwert
means of payment – Zahlungsmittel
measure – Maß
measure of capacity – Hohlmaß
medieval – mittelalterlich
membership number – Mitgliedsnummer
merchant – Händler, Handels~
miner – Minenarbeiter
minimum connecting time – Mindestumsteigezeit
mistress – hier: Frauchen
mobile phone – Mobiltelefon
modem hook-up – Modemanschluss
mode of transport – Transportart
mother and child compartment – Mutter-Kind-Abteil
mug – (Kaffee-)Pott
mushroom – Pilz
myriad – große Menge

**N**

nanny – Kindermädchen
nap – Nickerchen
native – Einheimischer
negotiate, to – verhandeln
nickname – Kosename

**O**

oak – Eiche
obligation – Verpflichtung
occasional – gelegentlich
occupancy – Belegung
occupation – Beruf
occupy, to – belegen
ocean view – Meerblick
offer – Angebot

| | |
|---|---|
| office hours | – Bürozeiten |
| on duty, to be | – im Dienst sein |
| onset | – Beginn |
| on-site representative | – Zielgebietsvertreter |
| on time | – pünktlich |
| onward connection | – Weiterverbindung |
| open-plan car | – Großraumwagen |
| operate, to | – betreiben |
| operator | – Vermittlung |
| optional | – freiwillig |
| orbit, to | – umkreisen |
| origin | – hier: Abflugort |
| outline | – Gliederung |
| outrigger | – Ausleger |
| overnight stay | – Übernachtung |
| overweight | – übergewichtig (Gepäck) |
| owing to sth | – aufgrund |

**P**

| | |
|---|---|
| package holiday | – Pauschalreise |
| parlo(u)r | – Salon |
| passenger's aid | – Bahnhofsmission |
| peak | – Gipfel |
| permission | – Erlaubnis |
| Personal Accident and Effects Insurance (PAE) | – Insassenversicherung |
| pharmacy | – Apotheke |
| picture window | – Panoramafenster |
| pilgrim | – Pilger |
| pillow | – Kissen |
| plaster | – Pflaster |
| platform | – Bahnsteig |
| pleasure | – Vergnügen |
| port | – Hafen |
| porter (BE) | – Gepäckträger |
| porthole window | – Bullauge |
| post | – hier: Stelle |
| post code | – Postleitzahl (GB) |
| precaution | – Vorsichtsmaßnahme |
| preference | – Vorliebe |
| present, to | – präsentieren |
| presentation | – Vortrag |
| printer | – Drucker |
| proceed, to | – hier: weitergehen |
| producer | – Leistungsträger |
| prohibit, to | – verbieten |
| prohibition | – Verbot |
| property | – Besitz |
| protection | – Schutz |
| provide, to | – zur Verfügung stellen |
| purchase, to | – kaufen |
| purpose | – Zweck |
| purser | – Zahlmeister/Chefsteward |
| put somebody through, to | – jmd. verbinden mit |

**Q**

| | |
|---|---|
| quad | – 4-Bett-Zimmer |
| questionnaire | – Fragebogen |
| queue | – (Warte-)Schlange |
| quote, to | – hier: angeben |

**R**

| | |
|---|---|
| rails (BE) | – Gleis, Schienen |
| rebook, to | – umbuchen |
| receive, to | – empfangen |
| receiver | – Hörer |
| recipient | – Empfänger |
| recline, to | – zurücklehnen |
| recommend, to | – empfehlen |
| record, to | – aufzeichnen |
| recover, to | – hier: wiederbeschaffen |
| reduction | – Minderung |
| reference | – Bezug, Empfehlung |
| refreshment | – Erfrischung |
| regular | – regelmäßig |
| reimburse, to | – entschädigen |
| relieve, to | – entbinden von |
| renewal | – Erneuerung |
| rent, to | – mieten |
| rental car | – Mietwagen |
| rental contract | – Mietvertrag |
| rental terms | – Mietbedingungen |
| replete with | – reichlich ausgestattet mit |
| reply | – Antwort |
| request, to | – anfragen |
| require, to | – benötigen |
| requirement | – Erfordernis |
| reserve | – Reservat |
| responsible, to be | – verantwortlich sein |
| restaurant car | – Speisewagen |
| restful | – erholsam |
| restroom | – Toilette |
| résumé | – Lebenslauf (USA) |
| retire, to | – hier: in den Ruhestand treten |
| return flight | – (Hin- und) Rückflug |
| revenue | – Einnahmen |
| rosemary | – Rosmarin |
| round out, to | – abrunden |
| round trip | – Hin- und Rückflug |
| rude | – unfreundlich |
| rural | – ländlich |

**S**

| | |
|---|---|
| safety standards | – Sicherheitsstandards |
| salary | – Gehalt |
| salmon | – Lachs |
| saloon car (BE) | – Limousine |
| salutation (line) | – Anrede(-zeile) |
| satisfaction | – Zufriedenheit |
| scale(s) | – Waage |
| schedule | – (Flug-)Plan |
| scheduled air service | – Linienflug |
| scheduled flight | – Linienflug |
| scone | – engl. Gebäck |
| scooter | – Motorroller |
| scrambled eggs | – Rührei |
| scuba diving | – Tauchen |
| secluded | – abgeschieden |
| section | – Bereich |
| sedan (AE) | – Limousine |
| senior citizen | – älterer (Mit-)Bürger |
| setting | – Schauplatz |
| settle, to | – hier: klären |
| shipping company | – Reederei |
| shore | – Ufer |
| side dish | – Beilage |
| significant(ly) | – bedeutend |
| single (room) | – Einzelzimmer |
| single flight | – Hinflug |
| skill | – Fertigkeit |
| sleek | – schlank |
| sleeping car | – Schlafwagen |
| slide | – Dia |
| smooth | – glatt, weich |
| snorkeling | – Schnorcheln |
| snow-capped | – schneebedeckt |
| source | – Quelle |
| spa | – (Heil-)Bad |
| spark, to | – versprühen |
| sparkling water | – Mineralwasser |
| splendid | – herrlich |
| spouting geysers | – speiende Geysire |
| spring | – Quelle |
| stagecoach | – Postkutsche |
| stagnant | – stehend |
| stalk | – Pirsch |
| stargaze, to | – in die Sterne schauen |
| starter | – Vorspeise |
| state-of-the-art | – hochmodern |
| stateroom | – Kabine |
| station wagon (AE) | – Kombiwagen |
| steam-engine | – Dampfmaschine |
| stern | – Heck |
| stopover | – Zwischenstopp |
| subject (line) | – Betreff(-zeile) |
| subject to, to be | – unterworfen sein |
| submit, to | – unterbreiten |
| subway | – hier: U-Bahn |
| suggest, to | – vorschlagen |
| suit, to | – hier: entsprechen |
| sumptuous | – üppig |
| superior | – höherwertig |
| Supplemental Liability Insurance (SLI) | – Zusatzhaftpflicht-versicherung |
| supply, to | – bereitstellen |
| support, to | – unterstützen |
| suspend, to | – einstellen |

**T**

| | |
|---|---|
| take off, to | – starten |
| take-off | – Start |
| tarragon | – Estragon |
| tax | – Steuer |
| temper, to | – temperieren |
| temperate | – gemäßigt |
| terminus/termini (pl) | – Kopfbahnhof/-höfe |
| terrific | – sagenhaft |
| third-party insurance | – Haftpflichtversicherung |
| ticketing | – Tickets ausstellen |
| timetable | – (Flug-)Plan |
| tinted | – getönt |
| tip | – Trinkgeld |
| tire (AE)/ tyre (BE) | – Reifen |
| tour guide | – Reiseführer |
| tourist board | – Fremdenverkehrsamt |
| tour operator | – Reiseveranstalter |
| trace back, to | – zurückverfolgen |
| track (AE) | – Gleis, Schienen |
| trademark | – (Handels-)Marke |
| trainee | – Praktikant |
| travel agent | – Reisemittler |
| travel benefit | – Reisevergünstigung |
| travel requirements | – Reiseanforderungen |
| traveler's aid (AE) | – Bahnhofsmission |
| triple (room) | – 3-Bett-Zimmer |
| trolley | – hier: kleiner Bus |
| turning | – Abzweig |
| turn-of-the-century | – Jahrhundertwende |

**U**

| | |
|---|---|
| unforeseen | – unvorhersehbar |
| unique | – einzigartig |
| unspoiled | – unberührt |
| urban | – städtisch |

**V**

| | |
|---|---|
| vaccination certificate | – Impfbescheinigung |
| valid | – gültig |
| validity | – Gültigkeit |
| variety | – Auswahl |
| vehicle | – Gefährt |
| Victory Column | – Siegessäule |
| voluntary | – freiwillig |

**W**

| | |
|---|---|
| wade, to | – waten |
| waive, to | – verzichten auf |
| wall news-sheet | – Wandzeitung |
| wastepaper bin | – Papierkorb |
| weight | – Gewicht |
| weightlessness | – Schwerelosigkeit |
| whisper, to | – flüstern; hier (poet.): säuseln |
| word-processing program(me) | – Textverarbeitungs-programm |

**Y**

| | |
|---|---|
| yellow pages | – Branchenbuch |
| YMCA: Young Men's Christian Association | – Christlicher Verein Junger Menschen |
| yours faithfully | – Mit freundl. Grüßen |
| yours sincerely | – Mit freundl. Grüßen |
| yours truly | – Mit freundl. Grüßen |

**Z**

| | |
|---|---|
| ZIP (Zone Improvement Plan) code | – Postleitzahl (USA) |